THE SUN TYRANT

THE SUN TYRANT

A NIGHTMARE CALLED NORTH KOREA

JP FLORU

FOREWORD BY JACOB REES-MOGG MP

\Bb\

Biteback Publishing

First published in Great Britain in 2017 by
Biteback Publishing Ltd
Westminster Tower
3 Albert Embankment
London SE1 7SP
Copyright © JP Floru 2017

ISBN 978-1-78590-221-5

10 9 8 7 6 5 4 3 2 1

A CIP catalogue record for this book is available from the British Library.

Set in Minion Pro

Printed and bound in Great Britain by
CPI Group (UK) Ltd, Croydon CR0 4YY

A devastating report by the Commission of Inquiry established by the United Nations Human Rights Council concluded that the North Korea government has committed systematic human right abuses at a scale without parallel in the contemporary world – including extermination, murder, enslavement, torture, imprisonment, rape, forced abortions and other sexual violence.

HUMAN RIGHTS WATCH 2015

To the 25.6 million prisoners in North Korea,
who one day will be free.

And to E., and great and wonderful things.

CONTENTS

FOREWORD

North Korea has a political system as evil as any the world has ever seen. It has installed concentration camps where people are sent to work until they die. It has a policy that led to a famine which may have killed millions and has had long-term health effects on many more. And it permits the murder of anyone who seems to oppose the regime in any way.

Beyond the border, it is easy to see the Kim family, especially Kim Jong-un, as simply comic. His funny haircut, the absurd language and the extraordinarily blatant propaganda make it difficult for the rest of the world to take the sheer evil of the man and his government seriously. The total control of people's lives and the cult-like status of the Kim family in North Korea, however, create prime conditions for the government to continue their tyrannical rule, while the erratic approach to foreign affairs, combined with the threat of nuclear war, enables them to squeeze money and supplies from foreign governments – not that any of it ever reaches the poverty-stricken civilians who so desperately need it.

In JP Floru's excellent travel diary, he exposes the horrifying extent of the Kims' brainwashing of their people. He observes (and, at the behest of his guides, reluctantly participates in) bowing to statues of the Kims and overhears instructions that saving a picture of the Kims from a burning building is more important than rescuing a child. Before visiting the embalmed body of Kim Il-sung – who, although dead, remains the eternal President of North Korea – the tour guide, who is more like a prison guard, checks every item of clothing, including a used Kleenex, to make sure that visitors are sufficiently respectfully dressed to meet the corpse.

The whole organised trip is a propaganda exercise, an effort of the minders to sell the delights of North Korea; yet the surreal totalitarianism present in all aspects of the visit can do little else but instill fear and alarm in the group. The residents, however, must accept the situation or risk not only their own liberty, but that of three generations of their family. This is where JP Floru's book is so well constructed. He draws out from the tourist experience the brutality of the Kims' regime, and clarifies the many points where invented history diverts from the bleak reality. The population is fed on lies that are accepted because they are forbidden any access to sources of the truth. Smuggling DVDs from China is punishable by a machine-gun firing squad, and anyone who expresses even remote disdain for the regime just disappears.

While it is easy to laugh at this fat little man in a boiler suit, as Jeremy Paxman so memorably put it, underestimating his depravity goes some way to cover up the horrific goings-on in North Korea. The West's assumption that he is mad has enabled him to play the West for fools; and even the Chinese government have been carried along by the manipulation of these so-called Great Leaders of North Korea.

It would be easy for a travel book about North Korea to be simply voyeuristic, but this is not the case here. JP Floru goes to great lengths to reveal the shocking reality of a country terrorised by its leader, offering the West much-needed insight into the atrocities that occur when the truth is rewritten beyond recognition.

Hon. Jacob Rees-Mogg MP

PREFACE

If I use the real names of the people I met in North Korea, they will not be seen again. And neither will their other halves. Nor their children. Nor their parents. Nor their brothers and sisters. That is how things work down there. I don't think it was particularly wise to put my own name on this book.

North Korea is the only country in the world where the rulers are not only a dynasty, but are also venerated as Gods. North Koreans are made to bow to the statues of their leaders for fear of being sent to a labour camp, and the façades of all public buildings carry gigantic photos of the Great Leaders. Children as young as six are taught in school to hate Americans, the Japanese and whoever else is singled out as a class enemy. During the famine in the late 1990s, international food aid was kept back for the elite and the army while the population was reduced to munching tree bark. The regime continues to build up its nuclear missile programme at great expense while the population starves. The current Great Leader, Kim Jong-un, announces his imminent annihilation of South Korea, the United States and Japan with jocular regularity.

There are no human rights. The Western Gregorian calendar has been replaced by the Juche calendar, in which 1912, the year President Kim Il-sung was born, is Year One.

Thankfully, the regime also provides some relative comic relief. In January, the Pyongyang *Times* claimed that North Koreans had discovered hangover-free alcohol that 'exudes national flavour without dampening your national fervour in the morning', and the year before, NK News announced that medicines containing extracts from the insam plant could cure SARS and AIDS.

I went to North Korea to run the Pyongyang marathon. Three friends were running it and had asked me to come along. I said yes – because travelling to the moon is not available yet. Then I realised they were going for only three days, and that the marathon trip would not include a visit to the Kims' Mausoleum, so I switched to a nine-day tour instead. I also decided not to run the marathon myself, but to go along as a mere spectator. I did not want to risk blisters at the start of a tour; and North Korea is not a place where you want to end up in hospital.

Those who know me well all expected me to get into trouble with the authorities. 'Please don't say or do anything you will regret,' my mother begged me. My friend John was nearly in tears, while Jimmy promised he would set up the 'Free JP Campaign'.

It wasn't the best of times to visit the shifty kid in the class, since North Korean leader Kim Jong-un chose this precise moment to test a few ballistic missiles. Most just flopped into the sea as per usual, but Kim called it a great triumph and President Obama promptly signed new sanctions to punish the sanctions-infested pariah state. A few weeks before I left, 21-year-old American student Otto Warmbier was arrested for pinching a propaganda poster from the hotel where we were going to stay. His sentence of fifteen years' hard labour caused consternation the world over.

The icing on the cake was Kim Jong-un's announcement a few days before my departure that a new famine was coming (after his announcement, he attended a 1,000-chefs' cooking competition). My mother was now calling me every day to dissuade me from going, but my marathon friends and I just made a last-minute dash to the supermarket to fill all the remaining nooks and crannies with chocolate and nutritious bars.

I had not set out to write a book. But even as little as nine days in North Korea gave me such a tsunami of material that I could not resist the challenge.

CHAPTER ONE

NORTH KOREANS DON'T EAT GRASS (OR DO THEY?)

'If you are arrested, there is nothing we can do for you,' the guidelines from the British Embassy laconically stated. Their advice was hidden in the ten pages of dos and don'ts that we received from the travel agency in Beijing.

That was not the end of it. We spent the entire morning of our arrival in Pyongyang receiving an even more extensive briefing about the rules.

'Sometimes you will see people on the side of the road cutting grass with scissors. Please do not misunderstand. They are not going to eat it! It is to feed their rabbits.' Our guide laughs encouragingly, while keenly observing us.

None of us join in. Never mind people eating grass: do they actually cut it with scissors? Most of us have read up for this trip, so we know that during the famine in the 1990s, North Koreans definitely ate grass. Tree bark, too.

She pauses. Then our guide continues:

'When there is a photo of the Great Leaders on the cover of a newspaper, make sure not to fold it in the middle of the photo, because that is disrespectful. Also, do not throw the paper on the floor. You will be reprimanded if you do. Just give it to us, and then we will dispose of it.'

I quickly decide not to touch papers featuring the leaders' images. When the German architect Philipp Meuser produced an architectural guide to Pyongyang a few years ago, it was blacklisted by the regime because it had a double-page photo of a statue of the Leader across the centrefold.

It's not just the photos that are a sensitive issue: the Great Leader's name must always be spelled as one word on one line; it may not be split over two lines. And just to make sure that you don't miss out on the really important stuff in North Korean publications, the Great Leaders' names are always printed in bold.

'Some things may be different in your own country. In the next days we will go to the statues of the Great Leaders. You will be expected to bow and lay flowers, as a show of respect. Please follow the rules, yes?'

The detailed instructions as to what is not permitted go on and on. When visitors leave the country, border guards check their cameras, delete photos and make arrests at will. The truth is that most visitors are so terrified of the consequences that they stay well clear of even innocuous acts. In North Korea, never to be heard of again is, well, not unheard of.

'We will tell you when you can take photos. Do not take photos of ordinary people without their permission: they will react very badly if you do. Also, do not take photos of building sites, or inside shops, or of housing. These may give the wrong impression about our country. Do not take photos of anything relating to the military. Those are our rules. In your own countries you have rules, too.'

She gives us a broad smile, as if we are about to receive free kittens. Then her face turns serious again.

'Is there anybody here who is American, who has family who fought in the Korean War, or who has family living in Korea?' she asks.

'I am American,' a small voice comes from the back. Natasha is a plucky redhead who everybody instantly likes.

'We will have a word with you later. But for all the others: please do not express political views while you are in the DPRK. Also, do not express religious views. No proselytising, please!'

In the coming week we never see Mrs Kim as serious as she is on that first day. She makes it clear that if we misbehave, we risk being arrested and thrown out of the country. Not only that, but our minders' lives will be well and truly ruined as they will be held responsible for what we do. And it doesn't just affect *they themselves*, since in North Korea, an offence against the state contaminates the entire family. Just like Adam and Eve's original sin, it is passed on through the generations.

But I'm jumping ahead. The mad adventure started a few hours earlier. The Air Koryo plane from Beijing to Pyongyang was like any other, apart from the TV screens in the seats that showed a thirty-minute political propaganda film on a loop with no button to switch it off. The Great Leader smiles, the masses applaud, tanks five abreast thunder through streets and missiles are launched; and the whole spectacle is accompanied by soothing lounge music, just like an advert for deodorant.

The new Pyongyang Airport was completed only last year. It's spotless and very large, but oddly, we are the only visitors. No other planes arrive; no other planes are parked outside; and apparently nobody is going to depart today either. Do they make sure that foreigners don't exchange intel by leaving a day or two between each arrival or departure?

Very few tourists venture here. According to North Korean government figures, about 80,000 Chinese and about 20,000 other tourists visited in 2015. The US Department of State still 'strongly recommends against all travel to North Korea'. For the UK Foreign Office, North Korea is not off-limits, but it states that 'the level of tension on the Korean peninsula can change with little notice' and that 'offences that would be considered trivial in other countries can incur very severe penalties'. Despite these warnings and Kim Jong-un's threats to 'turn South Korea into a sea of fire', the Great Leader has joyfully announced that 1 million tourists shall visit the country by the end of 2017, and 2 million by 2020. A number of glamorous attractions such as 'package holidays for the seaside' offering ski resorts, a water park and 'fun fairs with roller coasters, fast food stands and a 5-D theatre' are sure to lure Western punters away from the Costa del Sol to Kim Jong-un's welcoming bosom. But there are even better crowd-pleasers: 'a new high-tech shooting range where visitors can hunt animated tigers with laser guns or use live ammo to bag real pheasants, which can be prepared to eat right there on the spot'.

The command of the Supreme Leader has not been heeded by the Western capitalist traitors yet. I guess the risk you run of being shot – like the South Korean tourist who strayed off a path in the mountains into a security zone in 2008 – doesn't help to push up the numbers.

The only other people in the arrival hall are soldiers and uniformed airport staff. All have splendid kepis that look like upturned Victoria sponges. On top of the slight frame of the average North Korean, the kepis are very large indeed.

'You can't believe anything you see,' Australian Pete warns me.

On the customs declaration form, you have to disclose the amount of currency you are carrying with you as well as the number of books, cameras and other electronic devices that you are bringing along. A soldier with an impressive kepi asks for my iPhone and commands me to unlock it before spending about ten minutes going through my photos and emails. Thankfully, and like everybody else, I have been in deleting-mode for the entire one-and-a-half hour flight from Beijing.

Aussie Andrew, who sat next to me on the plane, is not so lucky: they find a few comical photos of the Great Leader in his phone's trash box.

'This is very bad!' they shout, eyes firing daggers, wagging their gloved fingers in his face.

They grab him by the shoulders and drag him to a room in the back. The group minders are called in and look very grave.

In the end they let him through, but his phone is confiscated and the minders keep a very close eye on him for the rest of the trip.

'Going through our phones! Man,' a fellow traveller observes. 'It's like being raped.'

Another soldier with an impressive kepi beckons me to a separate room. I have to show them the four books I declared. They flick through them. My Ronald Reagan book is scrutinised in great detail. They are especially jittery about books in Korean and political books. And bibles. Bibles are a big no-no. We were told so by absolutely everybody.

My fear was unwarranted: they don't mind my books and lead me off to the next control booth. There I am asked for my passport. Down here, I'm officially an artist. Journalists and politicians are as big a no-no as bibles and mini-skirts and South Koreans. South Koreans are the only nationality they don't let in; never mind that 20 per cent of North Koreans have family members across the border. Occasionally a handful of family reunions are allowed by the North – usually in return for shiploads of food aid or just plain dollars.

And then I'm let through! In the vast arrival hall the spotless floor reflects us like a mirror. At the opposite far ends are two identical shops. When I try to buy water, I have to use sign language as in this international airport the uniformed staff don't speak English. English is taught only to a few reliable party members. Soldiers with impressive kepis hang about and glare at us while trying to look nonplussed and debonair with a cigarette in their hand.

In the middle of the hall, a TV is beaming images of the Great Leaders, military parades and missiles setting off into cloudless blue skies. Whenever the Leader comes on, the voiceover is one of hushed reverence. Now a meeting is shown, with medal-encrusted delegates clapping in sync.

It's too early for confidences or snide remarks within the group about what we see and hear. Our faces are inscrutable.

'Welcome to the DPRK!' our guide-minders say, smiling.

We look confused.

'Yes, in this country, we say DPRK! We are the Democratic People's Republic of Korea. Please do not say North Korea as we are the entire country, the real Korea. It is an insult to say anything different.'

Mrs Kim is a diminutive lady of about thirty-five with delicate round glasses, almost like a pince-nez. She is dressed in a striking black Chanel spin-off skirt suit. The dictator orders the population to dress well so that the country makes a favourable impression upon foreigners.

Our second guide is Mr Chong. He is on his first trip. He is skinny and pretty; he looks about eighteen, even though he is twenty-five; and his English is not great. Every day, he will be dressed in a black suit with a white shirt and a black tie. At first I think that this is his interpretation of 'chic' and that, just like Mrs Kim, he wants to stand out in this egalitarian world. Later I realise that this is just North Korea's 'Sunday best' and every non-uniformed official is dressed the same.

In North Korea, the state always allocates you *two* minders: one keeps an eye on the other. They are to report anything untoward to the State Security Department. They are faithful party members, who will show us only what the regime wants us to see. Those not worshipping at the altar of the divine Leaders are not let anywhere near treacherous foreigners.

Our minders have a routine: while Mrs Kim does all the talking, Mr Chong hovers behind us, looking at our reactions and making sure that we stay with the group. In the coming days, whenever I go on a little adventure of my own, he will come and find me, grab me by the arm and pull me back to the main group.

From a corner, a local camera man is filming it all. We dub him Kim Kubrick and we are told that we will have the opportunity to buy his tape at the end of our voyage. We quickly become suspicious that the footage is not just a memento for ourselves, especially after the third time of being shown political propaganda films containing images of hapless clapping and flower-laying foreigners intermingled with devotional scenes carried out by locals.

I take a seat in the front of our green bus. Outside the airport, a giant screen is beaming more footage of the Great Leaders and their heroic army to whoever crosses this empty car park.

The main roads into Pyongyang are wide and modern and clean. Were these built for traffic that never came? We see no graffiti and no litter. There is a steady trickle of buses and the odd chauffeur-driven black sedan, in which officials hide behind dark windows. Cars are to North Koreans what private jets are to Westerners. We recognise a few Japanese-made cars, but the locals are told that they are North Korean, and they carry Korean names on the boots and bonnets. The few buses are full of squashed, unhappy-looking locals. Virtually everybody else is on foot or rides a bicycle.

One factor that makes the Pyongyang streets weird to Western eyes is the complete absence of commercial publicity. There are no flashy billboards, apart from those featuring government announcements with slogans in the circle-and-lines alphabet that none of us can read. There are also no loud shop-fronts. In fact, you have to look closely to identify any shop: at street level they have ordinary glass doors and ordinary house windows and only by peering inside can you see that there is some form of commercial activity going on.

By and large, Pyongyang looks pleasant. There are flags everywhere: you can have them in any colour, as long as it's red. Clean-looking apartment blocks are dotted about in expansive green lawns or concrete squares. I once read in a book that 'Pyongyang is completely grey'. The regime must have read that too, because now all the apartment blocks have been painted in pastel colours. The peach, mint-greens, light ochres and electric-blues are quite pretty.

The architecture is not bad either. When the Eastern Bloc was still the Eastern Bloc, East German architects were flown in to do the drawings. Kim Jong-il himself wrote a book about architecture (he was an expert on architecture, as he was an expert in everything else). *On the Art of Architecture* is overflowing with wise ideas such as 'the necessity to avoid decadent reactionary bourgeois design' and 'architecture must reflect a revolutionary outlook'. Kim II also defended architectural excess, claiming that 'grand buildings stand witness to the Leader's greatness'. But for architects the world over, salvation occurred when the Guiding Sun Ray came up with this entirely original gem: 'The magnificence of grand monuments is expressed, first of all, through unusually large size; and secondly by way of vast numerical quantity.'

The architectural genius of Kim Jong-il was inherited by his son, the present Kim Jong-un. Just like his father, Kim III travels up and down the country to visit building sites to tell people how to do their jobs. This includes deciding that the misguided sods living there should be deported, as occurred in 2013 when Kim Jong-un gave on-the-spot guidance that the perimeters of the city of Musan needed to be transformed in order to become exemplary. 600 households situated within some 300m of Musan's perimeters were told to pack up.

One can only imagine the terror of builders and architects when the Supreme Leader's motorcade swoops by. After Kim III expressed his disappointment with the design of the new Pyongyang Airport at which we had just arrived, the architect disappeared. He may have been executed, but we will never know: just like in Orwell's *Nineteen Eighty-Four*, those who incur the wrath of the dictatorship become 'unpersons'. Not only do they disappear, but their names are retroactively expunged from historical records as well. Mentioning an unperson would be a Thought Crime, and he who mentions an unperson risks becoming an unperson himself.

Mrs Kim explains the uses of the buildings on our left and right through the coach's microphone. They are invariably public. Dimensions and capacities are given in precise numerical detail. For many decades North Korea has been obsessed with the idea that if only they have large buildings, the world will take note. When the famine started and the food rations shrank, the building spree of megalomaniac buildings continued as before. The regime has always taken great pains to explain that in North Korea, nothing is lacking, and the buildings are erected to prove it.

But how can a poor country afford all these monumental public buildings? To begin with, the building costs are minimal. Soldiers, or 'soldier-builders' as they are often called, are used as unpaid labour. The only costs to develop a site are the building materials and the food for the soldiers. Sometimes even food isn't provided and soldiers are supposed to fend for themselves. North Korea also borrows a lot. By 2012, the country's external debt had risen to $20 billion, even though that year Russia wrote off 90 per cent of North Korea's debt. North Korea defaulted on its debts in 1980 and 1987.

All buildings have allegedly been built at record speed. What they're like inside, we do not know. Speed campaigns are used by the dictatorship to finish constructions ever faster, usually to coincide with some communist anniversary. In the early days the regime imposed 'Chollima Speed' on the progress of building, referring to the winged horse from Chinese mythology. Back in 1957 under the Five Year Plan, the workers of the Kansong Steel Plant were told to produce 10,000 tons more steel from a factory with a capacity of 60,000 tons. Instead, 120,000 tons more steel was produced. The Kansong Steel Plant was subsequently renamed Chollima Steel Complex. One little detail is never mentioned, however: that when rational economic management was abandoned at the expense of speed and quantity, the quality of the steel plunged.

'This building was constructed in just twelve months,' Mrs Kim marvels, pointing at a gigantic, sleek design that could take off for another galaxy at any moment. The first two Kims are watching us from two enormous portraits above the portal.

'Our respected Leader Kim Jong-il visited here in 2008 and 2010.' She looks as if we should be pleased.

'They all lie, you know,' Pete whispers behind me.

Pyongyang is the main trump card of the regime. Only the best is good enough for Pyongyang. Indeed, the standard of living in Pyongyang is substantially higher than elsewhere, but only supporters of the regime are allowed to live there. All housing in North Korea is allocated by the state on the basis of your reliability.

Kim Jong-il regularly announces that Pyongyang is the most beautiful city in the world. I wouldn't go that far, but they certainly put on a good show. But a show is all it is. In his book *Architectural and Cultural Guide to Pyongyang*, Philipp Meuser summarises the city in three sentences: (1) Behind the clean residential blocks are primitive single-floor huts; (2) monuments to the Leaders and the party are well-lit at night, while the apartments next to them are in darkness; and (3) public buildings have marble façades, while the pavements are full of potholes and cracks.

Most people in the streets are demurely dressed in black, brown or grey. There do not appear to be homeless people or prostitutes: the police make sure of that. In the 1980s the dictatorship also decided that disabled people are a stain on Pyongyang. They were banished to the countryside.

Suddenly we catch sight of a few hundred women in pastel-coloured hoop-dresses walking away from a big official building. The tulle fabric expands in straight lines from the neck onwards, like upside-down ice-cream cones.

Mrs Kim explains: 'Those are called *hanboks*. It is the national dress in the DPRK! I have one, too. These women are going to practise for the night-time torch procession.'

Over the next few days, we will see *hanboks* again and again. What Mrs Kim does not tell us is that what one wears is state policy. Trousers were once seen as 'unbefitting' for women, but this edict is now largely ignored. When women were allowed only to wear skirts, they were also forbidden from riding bicycles in urban areas.

Skimpy clothing and tops with English words printed on them are definitely out. There was a time when wearing jeans, that epitome of Americanism, could land you in a concentration camp. Basically, anything that looks too foreign is suspect. The more that specific items of clothing are frowned upon by the regime, however, the more popular they become with rebellious youths. People watch South Korean films and TV shows on DVD, and they like what they see. North Korean fashion is distinctly uncool.

Occasionally new campaigns are launched to remind people

about the socialist sartorial requirements. Fifteen-year-old members of the Kim Il-sung Socialist Youth League happily operate as some sort of fashion police, roaming the streets and shaming 'subversives'. They also target people with the wrong haircut, such as styles where hair covers the ears; but more about hair later.

'You are so lucky! Today is the day that the Great Leader Comrade Kim Jong-il was elected Chairman of the DPRK National Defence Commission!' Mrs Kim sounds really excited; a little breathless even. Then she continues:

And one of you is even luckier! One of you has her birthday on the same day as our Eternal President Kim Il-sung on Friday! We will do something for that most auspicious event. I will not reveal who of you it is yet, but you know who you are, and you must be very happy!

The language North Korean officials use is often from a bygone era. There is a lot of communist jargon thrown around, and assorted official minders at the many buildings we visit somehow use it with a straight face. South Korea, for example, is never mentioned: officially it does not exist. 'Koreans in the south' are 'crying under the American yoke' and their 'puppet regime'. 'American imperialists' is the North Korean jargon for 'Americans'.

Kim Il-sung is called 'The Eternal President' and used to be known as 'The Marshal' (or, before he promoted himself, 'The General'). When his son Kim Jong-il became a Marshal as well, there was a risk of confusion. So his father obtained a promotion and became 'Generalissimo'. Kim Il-sung thereby became part of a select few, including Stalin, Mussolini and Franco. Kim Jong-un is now a Marshal too.

Kim Il-sung was also known as 'The Great Leader' and Kim Jong-il as 'The Dear Leader'. The regime claims that the title of 'Dear Leader' was the result of thousands of letters requesting the title received from ordinary North Koreans: 'The government eventually gave in to the will of the people.'

Besides many official titles, the Great Leaders also enjoy a large arsenal of grandiose self-attributed nicknames, which I will pepper throughout this book.

We drive around an impressive triumphal arch.

'We will visit this later,' Mrs Kim promises.

'On the right is Kim Il-sung Square!' she continues breathlessly. 'This is the main square, used for mass events. Sometimes 1 million people are involved. It is a great honour to take part, and the people do it because of their love for the Great Leader.'

Theatrical effect is key here, as it is everywhere. The end of the paved square disappears in the fog.

The bus drives fast, so we are only able to take some blurred photos of the thousands of people in rows performing acrobatics with red flowers made of wood.

'They are preparing the big torchlight procession,' Mrs Kim coos.

Is this copied from the ones Hitler held? Over the coming days we will see these rehearsals again and again. We have all seen the marches with choreographed thousands creating mass visual effects on YouTube or as the 'fancy that!' item during the last minute of the evening news. The locals spend an inordinate amount of time in their working days preparing for the mass events. Every other day they are called upon by the university, student or work groups, membership of which is compulsory. Participation in the rehearsals is not optional.

We cross a bridge to an island in the Taedong River, where our hotel is. There is no way one could make a quick night-time dash into the city, as you would either have to swim across or pass the checkpoint on the bridge. There are no other residential buildings on the island. We are told not to photograph the two massive construction sites we pass.

'Your hotel is called the Yanggakdo,' Mrs Kim announces.

A frisson of excitement snakes through the bus: it is here that barely four weeks ago the widely reported 'stolen-banner-incident' took place, which alarmed all our parents, family members and friends.

The spinal 47-floor building comes into view. On top is a round floor. The views must be breath-taking. We drive through the gate and into a fenced-off area.

Please stay within the perimeter of the hotel. If you want to go out, tell your guides, and then one guide will go with you. There are certain areas where you can run to practise for the marathon, but one of us needs to accompany you. Also, please do not go to the fifth floor!

'Why?' a brave person shouts from the back of the bus.

'That is the area for the cleaners. Some think it is for spying or something, but in reality it is nothing of the sort. It is just an area for cleaners!' She laughs as if she just said something extremely funny.

'You can't believe anything,' Pete stage-whispers for the third time. People in the group exchange knowing glances.

The incident is fresh. As I mentioned before, American student Otto Warmbier was condemned to fifteen years' hard labour for stealing a propaganda poster from the off-limits fifth floor of our hotel just one month earlier.

There is a whole sub-culture out there of foreign travellers trying to get access to it. In the lift the button for the fifth floor is missing. According to the daredevil ninjas who brag about it on the web, you can reach it by walking down the fire-escape stairs from the sixth floor. I've seen the photos taken by some who sneaked in there: the corridors have grey concrete walls with communist propaganda posters. The doors are made of steel and are locked. Some claim they have seen guys huddled over monitors and using headphones. Others say they saw a pile of redundant listening devices in the corridor. Whatever the truth is, I have no desire to be locked up in the gulag for the privilege of seeing the floor myself. My mother will be relieved. And this is probably why the excessive punishment of the hapless American happened: to warn foreigners to stay within the confines of North Korean law. In the next few days, I cannot help but notice how many North Koreans in dark suits with Workers' Party badges leave and enter the lifts on the sixth floor.

Now Josh takes over. Josh is the American who is the representative of the Chinese travel agency with whom we have booked this trip. He says he is a student perfecting his Mandarin in Shanghai. He is about twenty-seven or so with a crew cut and trustworthy grey eyes. He always remains even more guarded than the North Korean minders. Being an American, he must be treading on eggshells in this part of the world. He refuses to partake in any political discussion, even when I ask him such an anodyne question as who he voted for in the last American presidential election. He usually takes charge of practical arrangements; in other words, he is responsible for making sure that everybody turns up on time.

'We will go straight to lunch in the main dining hall. And this afternoon we will leave from the parking lot at 3 o'clock. Please always arrive on time. The hotel is very busy; there are 600 people staying to run the marathon, and the lifts can get a little crowded. Provide at least twenty minutes for use of the elevators. It wouldn't be the first time the bus left without a group member who was still waiting for a lift on the fortieth floor.'

He pauses to let it sink in.

'There are several restaurants, but we will use the main banqueting hall on the ground floor to your left. Did you see that the top floor is round? That's the revolving restaurant: check it out. When you go in, on the left of the reception desk is the entry to the Korean basement, which has a swimming pool. On the right is the Chinese basement.'

He continues with a mischievous grin: 'In the Chinese basement you can have a massage.' He leaves a pregnant pause. 'Sometimes it goes beyond a mere massage.'

The banqueting hall is about 20m by 60m and can easily seat 500 diners. The room is crowded with a United Nations of marathon runners. There are no fewer than four long buffet tables with food warmers carrying copious plates of identical piles of bland food. It's a far cry from the dry baguettes and five-month-old croissants some visitors are allegedly given in more remote North Korean hotels (one friend recounted how his hotel in the north had a full counter with delicious food on display, which transpired to be plastic and not available in its edible equivalent). There are plates of vegetables, fried tofu, overcooked fish, boiled potatoes, boiled rice, soup, chicken, bread and cold fats with some forlorn meat attached.

'What is that?' I ask Australian Pete, who seems knowledge-able about all things Asian. I point at a plate with pink, glutinous food.

'That is kimchi!' he says, with tinkling eyes and a naughty smile.

'Tell me more?'

'It's fermented cabbage. The guys here eat mainly kimchi and rice and not much else. I wouldn't take it, if I were you. It's a bit of an acquired taste, shall we say.'

The most shocking part of the buffet is the vast quantities. This will be repeated everywhere we eat in the coming days. There is always so much that three-quarters or more remains untouched.

Often you wouldn't want to eat it anyway: North Korean cuisine seems to focus on the bland and the filling. Nothing is seasoned, as government instructions tell chefs that Westerners won't like it. The mediocrity is odd because in South Korea, the best restaurants are those that serve North Korean specialities.

Just two weeks earlier Kim Jong-un told the population 'to prepare to chew on roots of plants once again'.

This figure of speech refers to the 1990s when millions of North Koreans died from hunger. Nobody quite knows how many died as the census conveniently stopped being carried out in 1993. The estimates vary from between 2.5 per cent of the population to 15 per cent. Even at the modest 2.5 per cent, the death toll would be comparable to the famine in China that resulted from Mao's 'Great Leap Forward'. As a proportion of the population, the North Korean famine may have been the most severe in Asia of the past fifty years. Some say the famine ended only when so many had died that the remaining had enough food to survive.

It is often stated that the North Korean famine was caused by 'natural disasters'. In reality, the famine was caused directly by the Kims' economic policies. With its harsh climate, North Korea has only a limited amount of fertile land. A normal economy would import the shortfall, but the North Korean regime imposes the Juche ideology of self-reliance: North Korean farmers are supposed to feed the entire nation. In the past, much was achieved by way of chemical fertilisers. To produce these, however, you need working factories. When the Soviet Union stopped being communist and wanted market rates for its fuel, North Korea couldn't afford it, so its fertiliser-producing factories stopped operating.

Kim Jong-il subsequently ordered an increase in production by way of a nationwide cutting down of the trees on the hills to allow for terrace farming. This deforestation caused flash-floods the next year that destroyed the crops on 15 per cent of all arable land. As there was no fuel, it was not possible to transport the remaining food to the areas most severely hit.

Kim then commanded farmers to hand over an even larger share of their crops to the state than before. Farmers did what farmers always do on such occasions: they started hoarding. The World Food Programme estimated that in 1996 half of the country's corn crop was kept back. Kim sent in the army to guard the fields from the farmers who worked them, but for a bag of potatoes or beans the poverty-stricken soldiers were all too happy to look away.

When the size of the catastrophe he had caused became apparent, Kim Jong-il had his agricultural minister Seo Gwan Hee executed by firing squad. Seo was accused of being a spy for 'the American imperialists and their South Korean lackeys' and of having sabotaged North Korea's self-reliance in agriculture. Several thousand spectators were rounded up to watch the execution.

The famine was used as an excuse for a good old purge against 'spies within'. Kim's brother-in-law Jang Song-thaek was put in charge of the clean-out. The regime found quite a clever little way to get rid of all those fellow citizens it didn't like. Every North Korean has an identification booklet from birth in which all his moves are recorded. These booklets often contain gaps; for example, about the whereabouts of citizens during the Korean War when the bureaucratic repression was in chaos. These gaps were now used as 'evidence' to purge 'spies'. Often prosecutors took revenge on their personal enemies. Moon Sung-sul, General Secretary of the Workers' Party, was tortured and beaten to death. Kim Yong-ryong, the Ministry of State Security's first Secretary, killed himself when agents burst into his room. Some 20,000 cadres, soldiers, security personnel, scholars and authors were sent to concentration camps. Many died. When matters got out of hand, those doing the purging were purged (not Kim's brother-in-law, rest assured) and some detainees were released. The lucky ones made sure to express their gratitude to the 'magnanimous' Kim Jong-il publicly.

When humanitarian aid started to arrive, the regime stole it. Between 1996 and 2001, North Korea received almost 6 million tons of food. More than half came from the American 'imperialists', the South Korean 'traitors' and the Japanese 'war criminals'. Between 2002 and 2007 it again received more than 5 million tons. Because of yet another nuclear crisis, the USA had reduced its aid by then, but South Korea made up for the shortfall and donated half of the total.

The international aid organisations were not given any control over who received the food. The aid was carted off upon arrival to feed the army and those friendly to the regime. The high-ranking defector Jang Jin-sung recounts in his acclaimed book *Dear Leader* how he, one of the chosen Pyongyang elite who worked for the propaganda department, was surprised when they received extra rations that consisted of American cheese, butter, olive oil etc. Defectors to South Korea who served in the army have also confirmed that they received food rations from South Korean aid. The quantities they received were so large that they couldn't eat it all, so they sold the surplus on the black market in exchange for foreign currency.

The dictatorship never admitted to its people that it received foreign food aid.

The rationing of all food to all North Koreans by way of the Public Distribution System gradually declined, until it came to a complete halt. Between 1994 and 1999 the monthly rations were cut by 70 per cent. By the end of that period, only 6 per cent of the population still received food rations. Food distribution was prioritised to the areas where the Reliable Class lives. The border regions, where typically the 'hostile' class lives, received virtually nothing. The government told the population that it was holding back food for starving South Koreans. At other times they claimed that the American imperialists had introduced a blockade.

Campaigns were launched to tell people how to deal with the shortages. One such campaign urged the population to eat less under the slogan, 'Let's only eat two meals a day!' In some places, methamphetamines were distributed to suppress appetite. Hordes of emaciated people scavenged further and further into the countryside for berries and mushrooms. They peeled the bark from trees and made a paste of negligible nutritional value from the soft layer beneath. Many sold all their possessions to pay for whatever food they could buy. Some even tried to sell their children in the hope that the buyer would take care of them. People became accustomed to walking around dead bodies on the street without looking back. In many towns a special corpse division was set up to pick up dead bodies from the streets.

There were even darker rumours: whispers to avoid eating meat soup from street vendors and warnings to children not to venture out alone at night. People went insane from hunger. It is believed that some killed and ate their infants. There were public executions for cannibalism. Stories like these are difficult to print as we can't quite believe anyone could sink that low. But there are other historical examples where this happened: during the famine created by Mao's Great Leap Forward (1958–61) there were incidents of cannibalism as well.

North Koreans survived by ignoring the communist laws forbidding private commerce. People started to trade to earn some extra income, even though this had been illegal for forty years. They were fast learners: in some areas water supply to houses ceased, and tap water was sold in the markets.

The regime did not sit back quietly while people attempted to feed themselves by way of 'selfish capitalism'. Public execution by firing squad was introduced for those caught hoarding food and 'gossiping' (i.e. talking about the famine: the words 'hunger' and 'famine' are banned in North Korea because they are seen as criticism of the state). *Nothing to Envy*, the excellent book by Barbara Demick about real lives in North Korea, describes a public execution in the northern city of Chongjin during the famine. A poor sod stole some copper wire from electric poles to sell for food.

For days, sound-trucks encouraged people to attend the execution and, on the fateful day, the heads of the neighbourhood committees knocked on people's doors and commanded them to attend. I assume copperwire theft declined after this.

Today, Pyongyang has just announced a nationwide campaign to save food. Everyone in the country must hand over two kilos of rice a month to the state warehouses. Farmers must 'donate' some of their meagre crops to the army. The official paper of the Workers' Party of Korea has warned its readers that even when they are starving to death, their loyalty to Kim Jong-un must be unwavering. It is estimated that about 10 million North Koreans are currently suffering from malnutrition. The average life expectancy in North Korea is ten years shorter than in South Korea.

And so, at every meal, we have a gnawing feeling of guilt when we leave three-quarters or more on our plates. Several accounts by Westerners who visited or lived in Pyongyang at the height of the famine confirm that even at that time, their hollow-eyed staff served them far too much food. The regime wanted to prove that, notwithstanding the propaganda of the American imperialists and their South Korean lackeys, all was hunky-dory in the DPRK.

CHAPTER TWO

WOMEN: TAKE CARE OF YOUR HUSBAND'S HAIRSTYLE

The Victorious Fatherland Liberation War Museum, which commemorates the 1950–53 Korean War, is of the awe-inspiring megalomaniac type that we will come to expect in this country. We get off the bus at a giant arch with a square behind it that is the size of several football pitches. Bronze statues of 'heroic' machine-gunning soldiers are dotted across the landscape as far as we can see. We are told that it will be OK to take photos, but not inside the museum.

An official minder in army uniform with an impressive kepi welcomes us. She has permed hair; in fact, all official minders have permed hair, as North Koreans are told to have 'traditional hairstyles compatible with socialism and the taste of the era'. Middle-aged women need to have short hair that can be permed, whereas young women can wear it longer, provided it's tied back.

The regime frowns on hairdos that 'stand witness to nascent capitalism and treacherous Westernisation'. At one point, state TV beamed out a much-ridiculed documentary called *Let's Cut Our*

Hair in Accordance with the Socialist Lifestyle. It exhorted Koreans to opt for one of several sanctioned hairstyles. You can find episodes on YouTube, but in the meantime, this is a literal transcript of one part:

[A woman's voice speaks in Korean, subtitled in English.]

Look at this petty person. This person named Ri Seokpok is a resident of Kwanmun-dong. Like now he has this disgraceful haircut came to Pyongyang for a business trip.

[This is illustrated by way of a photo of a man with a perfectly acceptable hairdo.]

Some unruly-haired people captured on camera meanly ran away, while other made excuses about being busy to get a trim.

[Photos of several men with perfectly acceptable hairdos.]

The TV program has criticised this one long-haired man's wife for not paying attention to her husband's hair.

[The backs of the heads of the husband and wife are shown. The husband has hair that reaches just above his shirt collar.]

This offender's excuse to the TV was that he had recently returned from a foreign business trip. But the program found another businessman who said, 'Whenever I go on overseas trips, I tidy myself in accordance with socialist lifestyle.'

[An 'educational' text headed 'Health' is now shown, accompanied by soothing background music.]

Excessive growth has negative effects on human intelligence development. Long hair consumes a great deal of nutrition, and could thus rob the brain of energy.

[Photo of man, with text underneath.]

The TV hold this man as exhibiting the correct haircut. It recommends 1–5cm for the back and sides and 5cm for the tops of head. Men over fifty are allowed up to 7cm to cover baldness. Visits to barber should be made every fifteen days.

[A quote from the state radio broadcast is shown in text, with soothing background music.]

Dressing in accordance with our people's emotion and taste: tidy attire is important in repelling the enemy's manoeuvres to infiltrate corrupt capitalist ideas and lifestyle and establishing the socialist lifestyle of military-first era.

[A quote from the state newspaper *Rodong Sinmun*.]

People who wear other's style of dress and live in other's style will become fools and that nation will come to ruin.

What the North Korean viewers thought of the programme is not recorded.

In 2013, Kim Jong-un published a list of photos with ten acceptable hairstyles for men and eighteen for women. In 2015 Kim decided that it would be a good idea if men copied his own bizarre hairstyle, which he labelled 'ambitious': it's combed back, presumably to give him some extra height. It is not compulsory to have it, but aspirational citizens have adopted it with gusto. The barbers in the capital have been doing a brisk trade since this announcement.

Our guide at the Victorious Fatherland Liberation War Museum seems unbothered by her imposed hairstyle. She smiles and lies cheerfully that she likes it. But surely lying requires a conscious act? She is only about thirty and chances are that she has never heard anything but the invented North Korean version of history. Is there, just like in Orwell's *Nineteen Eighty-Four*, a Ministry of Truth, which rewrites history after the facts? Indeed there is: it's called the Korean Central News Agency. It 'interprets' events. The guides' explanation of historical facts certainly makes one think of *Nineteen Eighty-Four*'s Newspeak, as they are both languages that say the opposite of what really happens to suit the Great Leaders' purposes. 'A lie told often enough becomes the truth,' Vladimir Lenin said. The communist dictatorships in the USSR, China and North Korea took note and duly rewrote history to underpin their claim of legitimacy.

It is difficult to repeat everything our guide said, but in DPRK-speak it came down to this: 'When the Japanese were defeated by Kim Il-sung's guerrilla fighters, Korea was divided along the Thirty-Eighth Parallel between the Soviets in the north and the American imperialists in the south. The Soviets withdrew and the DPRK became independent; the American imperialists stayed and continue to occupy part of Korea. In 1950 the American imperialists invaded the DPRK, but the DPRK resisted heroically and quickly occupied 90 per cent of the country. The American imperialists fought back. Eventually the American imperialists begged for mercy and were forced to sign the Armistice. It was a great victory for the Eternal President Kim Il-sung!'

I did not ask her how the war came to be portrayed as a victory, when the borders between the Koreas are pretty much the same as before the war.

The real history goes something like this: Japan deposed the last Korean king and annexed Korea in 1910. Korea was an access route to the minerals and industries of Manchuria. Japan built ports, industry and other infrastructure in North Korea, and kept the South as agricultural land.

After Japan was defeated by the Allies in September 1945, the Soviet Union and the USA divided Korea between them along the Thirty-Eighth Parallel. What to do with Korea was very much an afterthought: apparently US Secretary of State Edward Stettinius had to ask where Korea was.

The Soviets found a puppet president to run the North: Kim Il-sung, who had lived and been trained in the Soviet Union. Stalin then turned Mao into North Korea's lord (himself remaining the overlord, much like in feudal times).

Kim Il-sung was keen to conquer the South. He told Mao and Stalin that the Americans would be unwilling to defend South Korea, and that the South Koreans would rise up against the American imperialists as soon as a tank crossed the border. Stalin did not want a war with the USA, which was still the only nuclear power at the time. The Soviet Union was also bound by the pact with America that divided the Korean peninsula.

Mao offered to do the fighting. He had no pact with America, and he wanted to prove his worth to the Soviet Union and obtain much-needed military aid from it. In addition, he was keen to neutralise or establish victory over the USA. The USA still posed a hypothetical yet pertinent existential threat to his regime and Mao preferred to fight the USA on someone else's territory. In 1949 he gained absolute power over China and the Soviet Union exploded its first nuclear bomb. In January 1950, Stalin finally gave the green light.

In its surprise invasion North Korea conquered 90 per cent of the South, including the capital Seoul. The United States had resisted giving the South Korean army heavy weapons and tanks as they had feared that the fiercely nationalistic president Syngman Rhee would have been tempted to invade the North himself. For some reason, the Americans also thought that the South would be up to the challenge if invasion from the North came, even though South Korea had only 65,000 men under arms, whereas North Korea had 250,000. Left to fight the North Korean tanks, the South Koreans' only option was to organise suicide teams, which charged the tanks clutching explosives and grenades.

US General Douglas MacArthur led a United Nations coalition of twenty-one countries to take Korea back.* The North Koreans were routed, and the North Korean leaders abandoned Pyongyang and fled to the border. Mao feared that General MacArthur would march to Beijing. In the same month it conquered and occupied

---

* Interestingly, the Soviet Union did not use its veto in the UN Security Council to block this. In the history books this is routinely explained as having happened 'because the USSR was boycotting the United Nations at the time over Taiwan's continued occupation of China's seat as one of the five permanent members of the UN Security Council'. In fact, the reason was far more cynical. Stalin quite liked the idea of Western nations being tied down in a conflict in Korea, which was likely to be long because of the huge numbers of hapless soldiers China was willing to throw into the fray. It gave him a better hand to pursue his ambitions elsewhere. The USSR's representative at the UN, Yakov Malik, expressly asked Stalin whether he should return to exercise the veto over Korea in the Security Council. It would have been a small thing to turn up for this one precise vote, but Stalin told him to stay away.

Tibet, China started a massive counter-attack in Korea. Some 400,000 soldiers from the People's Liberation Army were rela-belled 'Chinese Volunteer Army', so the People's Republic would not *officially* enter into a war with the United States. They crossed the North Korean border to help the beleaguered friendly commu-nist regime. Mao cared little for the fact that his soldiers' chances of survival against the United Nations war machine were slim, especially since many were former soldiers of Chiang Kai-shek who had been taken into Mao's army after Chiang was defeated. A protracted war with liberal carpet bombing ensued.

Kim Il-sung realised he risked inheriting a wasteland and begged Stalin and Mao to sue for peace. By now Mao's general Peng Dehuai was firmly in charge of what remained of the North Korean army. It consisted of a mere 75,000 soldiers, which was small fry compared to the 450,000 Chinese 'volunteers'. Kim Il-sung quickly fell in line with Mao and agreed that continuing the war was the right course of action.

Mao's eagerness meant that the war lasted for another one-and-a-half years. About 90 per cent of North Korean infrastructure was destroyed. At one point, US Secretary of State Dean Rusk regret-fully observed that 'there was nothing left to bomb'.

The Armistice was signed between the United Nations and North Korea on 27 July 1953. A new border was drawn with a de-militarised zone in between that was to be policed by North Korea, South Korea and the United Nations.

An estimated 1.1 million people, both civilian and military, died in the war.

The museum here serves to prove that the Korean War was a great North Korean triumph. We are herded into a trench to admire captured weapons. A number of decommissioned tanks, guns, helicopters and aircraft taken from the United Nations' allies are shown in a hangar that is open for viewing on one side. Walking backwards ahead of us is our own Kim Kubrick, who is documenting our every nose-picking movement for posterity with his 1980s film camera.

'These tanks were taken by the glorious DPRK army and our Great Leader from the American imperialists and their puppets,' our uniformed minder drones.

She knows the invented history of the military booty by heart. Extra emphasis is put on the year of capture to show that many were captured years *after* the 1953 Armistice. In North Korea's invented history, the narrative of the 'continued aggressions' is key. The war is not over: American tanks could roll over the Thirty-Eighth Parallel at any moment now! The population must be prepared to confront the enemy. The lie legitimises the garrison economy: sacrifices must be made to withstand the coming onslaught. When at war, it is normal that individual liberty and democracy are suspended; therefore orders from up high must be followed without question. Disobedience is treason!

We turn right and there is the river and the USS Pueblo, an alleged US spy-ship that was taken by the North Koreans in 1968. On a wooden board are rudimentary plasticised photos of the eighty-two American seamen who were taken prisoner, as well as their signed and recorded 'confessions'. I don't think confessing is difficult when starvation in a concentration camp is the alternative. There is also a cringeworthy letter from the Lyndon Johnson Administration admitting wrongdoing and begging for mercy.

Inside the ship we are shown the 'spy room'. The machinery looks impressive, but I'm not an expert so I can't tell whether this is actual spy technology or just ordinary machinery. One of the ship's doors has the bullet holes from when the ship was captured and somebody has painted neat little red circles around the holes. It all feels a bit pathetic in its desperation to make a point.

The crème de la crème is the main museum. It is of truly gigantic proportions and is largely clad in gleaming marble with flashy gold detailing. Another minder has now taken over: she has the regulation socialist perm and is dressed in a long, black velvet robe with diamanté sequins.

'The museum was built in just ten months!' she proclaims in a strident voice.

The grand entrance hall with its dual staircase is a jaw-dropping example of just how much money this begging-bowl country is willing to pump into a museum of invented history.

Size is used to impress and inspire awe, a bit like Albert Speer's megalomaniac buildings for the Nazi regime. Giant multi-coloured crystal chandeliers remind the poverty-stricken populace that resistance is futile. The gigantic statue of Kim Il-sung at the end of the hall is bathed in a mysterious sunrise-evoking glow. It's a young, handsome Kim in a white dress jacket with golden buttons and epaulettes against a perfect, blue sky, with what appears to be fireworks behind him. We are made to bow. A head bow, as for HM The Queen, is not sufficient: we are talking bending one's body half-way at a forty-five degree angle for several seconds, until our minder stands up straight again and we know that it's permitted for us to follow suit. Thankfully, no photography or recordings are allowed inside, so Kim Kubrick can't film us.

We are shown a ten-minute black-and-white film titled *Who Provoked the Korean War*. The sentences of the voiceover sound wooden as if read aloud from Google Translate, with many mistakes and literary hyperbole. Special emphasis is paid to atrocities 'committed by the American imperialists'.

This is repeated ad nauseam on every wall in every one of the ninety other exhibition rooms of the museum. Images of maimed babies, burning buildings and slaughtered Koreans follow us around the building. There are some rather good renditions of bloody battles in oil on canvas. One large room displays mannequins of distressed Americans caught in a desperate impasse in a trench. Some are lying dead in the mud, with plastic vultures on poles ready for brunch.

One special exhibit is that of 'biological warfare by the American imperialists'.

'Containers with insects contaminated with these diseases were dropped from American planes,' our minder shouts.

On the wall are photos of beetles, spiders, rats and insects.

The story backfired badly at the time. The intel about this germ warfare came from Mao's military staff, and initially the Soviets believed it to be true. Internationally it was met with such incredulity that eventually even the Soviets disowned the story. There was never any actual evidence. Several Soviet generals who were in North Korea at the time later stated in interviews that there was no evidence of germ warfare whatsoever and that if it had existed, they would have known about it.

'This is the evidence!' our guide shouts, triumphantly pointing her baton at some jam jars with black goo inside.

North Korea's obsession with 'bacteriological warfare waged by the American imperialists' continues to this day. In the late 1980s the dictatorship's monthly magazine *Korea Today* alleged that the USA had dispatched a special unit of men infected with AIDS to South Korea to infect the population. They were also accused of exporting AIDS-infected blood.

'If you feel unwell or are in shock, do go sit in the hall,' our uniformed museum minder urges helpfully.

I wonder whether visitors get bonus points if they are 'overcome' by the horrors displayed.

At the end of our tour we are let into a huge, round cupola room at the top of the building. Around us on the wall is an entire 360-degree painting of the Battle of Taejon.

'Now you sit. We will see film,' the guide shouts.

We do as we are told and are all excited: we have no idea what precisely to expect, but the room is quite a spectacle; so a good show must be coming.

So we wait.

And wait.

Somewhere there is a hitch, but our minders show no anxiety.

The social media generation gets somewhat restless after a full five-minute wait.

We wait some more. Some of us giggle, nervously checking over our shoulders whether we are being observed. Whatever it is, the show is not starting.

And then it does! The platform on which we sit in the middle turns, and so the landscape on the wall scrolls past us. Lights in the painting go on to illustrate explosions, and there is the sound of cannons, guns and battle cries. It turns out to be a rather lame display. Then it's all over and the bright lights switch on. Our minders scrutinise our faces for evidence of awe.

When we get back on the coach, we again see groups of between 100 and 1,000 North Koreans, standing in circles and squares, apparently rehearsing the mass parades to come for the assorted birthdays of leaders and other parade-worthy commemorations. Quite a few are crouching on the ground and must be frozen stiff. Surely they are not freezing here of their own free will?

We pass an old gate-like building with a tiled pagoda roof. I excitedly ask whether we will be visiting this, the first 'old' (i.e. pre-communist) building we see. Mrs Kim dismisses my request with pursed lips. Have I just been categorised as 'difficult – to be watched'?

It is suddenly decided that we will visit the foreign language bookshop. The detour is exciting as it will allow us to go on a little 500m stroll through downtown Pyongyang!

We dismount from the bus. It is 6 p.m. and it is so cold that our ears nearly freeze off. The temperatures here are rather extreme: at midday it's 25 degrees and sunny, and you want to change into swim shorts; by six you risk frostbite. In winter, temperatures of minus thirty are not uncommon.

We are warned not to approach locals, because they 'will feel uncomfortable as they are not used to foreigners'. Nothing could be further from the truth. They seem mightily interested in us: always at least glancing and some even wave. At the same time they are reserved like the Japanese, and will keep staring until you look back, and then they usually quickly avert their eyes. But they need not fear: the dictatorship has duly informed them that the foreigners attending the marathon are here to express their affection and respect for Marshal Kim Jong-un. That is how foreigners' presence is always explained by the dictatorship.

'Do not take photos of the locals, they may become aggressive,' Mrs Kim warns, as if speaking of wild animals.

We of course all do, cameras dangling innocently from our necks, fingers on the buttons, snapping away blindly. As we are now walking close to the apartment blocks, instead of from the bus 100m away, we notice that they are not all as perfect as we first thought. There is a lot of flaking paint going on, with parts of render having fallen off and lying abandoned in heaps. Balconies are used to stow just about everything, which suggests that the flats are tiny. We are now approaching a building site.

'No photos!' Mr Chong shouts, alarmed.

The site is a heave of activity, with at least 100 workers scurrying around with bricks on their shoulders and wheeling wheelbarrows filled with cement. Rickety scaffolding, breaching all safety standards and seemingly held together with ropes, towers in the sky. Workers, building materials and the earth are all the same clay-brown colour.

Every crossroad is manned by a stern traffic warden, who is usually female. They stand in a white circle in the middle of the road and act as a human traffic light. They make pirouettes and rotating Nazi salutes: these must have been taught in traffic-warden-school as they all make the same movements wherever we go. When there is no traffic, which is most of the time, they still make robotic 180-degree turns every five seconds or so. Their vivid blue-green suits with impressively large, brass buttons and gold epaulettes are matched with black knee-length boots and an impressive kepi. It could be mistaken for a marshal's dress uniform. I guess it gives them pride in their job. Many ordinary jobs seem to warrant a gala uniform down here; indeed, about one in three pedestrians wears a military uniform. This is not so surprising: out of a population of 25 million, 9.5 million are in the army either as full-time employed, in military service, as paramilitary or as reserve soldiers. In 2001 it was suddenly decided that all civilians under forty, including students, have to enter compulsory military service for three years. The service is between seven and ten years long, and North Koreans are baffled when told that many countries do not have military service. Being forced into the army is not necessarily seen as a chore, as it may later give them easier access to the Korean Workers' Party membership and all the advantages that entails.

The bookshop is indistinguishable from residential buildings from the outside. It sells North Korean books, newspapers, magazines and small knickknacks you don't want. It's mainly the output of the three Great Leaders in English, French, Russian and some

Spanish. Kim Il-sung University reputedly stocks almost 100 books by the Great Leader. The titles here are fit for the communist-tyranny lending-library:

> *Kim Jong-il – The Great Man*
> *Kim Jong-il – Let the Entire Army, the Party, and All the People Conduct a Vigorous Forest Restoration Campaign to Cover the Mountains of the Country with Green Woods*
> *Kim Il-sung – Five Major Tasks of Party Cells*
> *Kim Jong-il – Let Us Hold the Great Leader in High Esteem Forever and Accomplish his Cause*

The current issue of the *Democratic People's Republic of Korea* magazine has a photo of a pink missile taking off on its front cover (the print colour may have gone wrong).

I buy a copy of *Supreme Leader Kim Jong Un in the Year 2013* as a prank for a friend. The chapters have riveting titles such as 'An arsenal for the agricultural front of socialism' and 'A day devoted to the strengthening of the Korean People's Army and happiness of the people'. It has lots of photos of the fat man with the strange hairdo giving on-the-spot guidance to experts twice his age. You can always see one or two soldiers hovering immediately behind him eagerly scribbling down every utterance in large notebooks.

On-the-spot guidance was a managerial style invented by his grandfather. The Leader ceaselessly travels the country to give detailed instructions to the farmers and workers on all subjects under the sun; and then the fount of all wisdom can claim credit for every achievement.

I am tempted to buy *Best Recipes of Pyongyang*. It is promising. Tangogi soup, for example, promises to be 'healthy, nutritious and digestible'. Phew! Other delicacies include aspic jelly of ox trotter – such a shame that the population can't obtain the ingredients. I also consider buying the autobiography of Kim Il-sung until I realise that it comes in eight volumes. While it would be interesting to compare the eight volumes with the invented history of North Korea to find out where the lies are, I am not prepared to carry the dead weight.

The prices, to be paid in Chinese renminbi, US dollars or euros, are high; it comes to about ten pounds for a book. Back in England, I wish I had bought more of these wacky titles. I could have made a quick buck, since there are virtually none available on eBay and those that come up sell for a multiple of the inflated Pyongyang prices.

'In half an hour we will have dinner in the restaurant,' Mrs Kim says when we are back at the hotel. 'It might be a good idea for you to go to bed early, as tomorrow you need to be fit to run the marathon.'

The regime has made sure that there is no valid excuse to leave the Janggakdo Hotel for a frolic of one's own: there is a bookshop, a souvenir shop, a bowling alley, a pool table room and a smelly supermarket where one can stock up on alcohol (including a not-too-bad Argentinian Chardonnay), cosmetics, plastic flowers, toilet paper and wet wipes. We had been told by the travel agency that we should bring toilet paper and wet wipes as such necessities would not always be available in North Korea. Strangely the rate at which dollars, euros and Chinese renminbi are accepted is very different from the rates we receive on the exchange markets in the West. The rates have been decided by the dictatorship: the less they like the country, the greater the variance is with world exchange rates. One gets very little for a dollar; a little more for euros; and renminbis are distinctly advantageous – I receive about 30 per cent more for it than what I paid in the UK. More than ever, North Korea is a parallel universe with a leadership from outer space.

I am curious about the rotating restaurant on the top floor. At some point the North Koreans acquired the know-how to build rotating floors on the top of buildings: this is not the only one. The 105-storey Ryugyong Hotel in central Pyongyang has five rotating restaurants on top. Whether they actually rotate is anybody's guess, as the hotel is still incomplete thirty-nine years after its construction commenced.

It takes me fifteen minutes to go up in the lift as it stops on so many floors. The restaurant is vast and empty but for the five staff who stare at me in surprise when the lift door opens. One enterprising waitress approaches, threatening me with a menu. She almost manages to push it into my hands but I retreat back into the lift. For the five seconds I was there, I was able to throw a glance out of the windows. Because it is dark outside (only the monuments to the Kims and the party are illuminated) and very bright inside (to suggest abundance, while at the same time exorcising the last scintilla of atmosphere), you cannot actually see anything of the no-doubt spectacular views. At night, the windows reflect like black mirrors.

My first instinct is to search for bugs, two-way microphones and cameras. Perhaps in the air vent high above the bed? I can't see any, but then I'm not a trained spy. My friend Lysander, who travelled to North Korea a few months ago, was luckier. He was staying in a room on the thirty-sixth floor of the Koryo Hotel. For some reason the hippie he shared a room with knew something about microphones and cameras. He unscrewed the front panel of the bedroom's radio speaker and there it was, dangling: a baby camera. With the many reported power cuts, one wonders how effective bugging would be.

My room on the twenty-fifth floor is fine; the bathroom is clean, the shower works and hot water runs. It is about 25 degrees though. Central Command has decided that 25 is just about the right heat. The authorities know best: one cannot control the temperature from the room. Unexpectedly, yet fortunately, the windows open.

I am lying in bed, wide awake. Not just because of the thumb-thumb-thumb of the building works at the public building next door that continues all night, but also because I've just realised I made a possibly fatal mistake. Here, in North Korea, I am officially an artist. You would have to be pretty dumb to admit that you are a writer or a journalist or a politician. But when my roommate Jacopo asked me what my profession was, I said I was a writer. I blurted it out before I thought of the bugs in the room. Will I find an AK47 against my temple in the middle of the night, be blindfolded and carted off in a green army lorry?

The procedure to come here was somewhat peculiar. Before you sign up and pay for a holiday in North Korea, you have to be approved by the regime. You basically apply to come here. So I filled in the form with my full name, passport number, nationality and profession. Three days later I received an email saying that I was approved and that I could now sign up for the trip.

But even that was somewhat peculiar: they told me that international payments for my trip should never mention North Korea or Pyongyang or Sunrise Tours, as such payments would be blocked under international sanctions. So payment goes to a travel agency in Beijing – which supposedly then pays the North Koreans. Sunrise Tours in Beijing then also made me sign a promise that I would ask for approval for anything I wrote about North Korea after my trip. Never mind free speech. Here we have a commercial business imposing Pyongyang's censorship.

And still I cannot sleep. I suddenly remember that I have not tried out the enigmatic basement Josh told us about. In the bed next to mine Jacopo is in a deep sleep. I move out of bed and tiptoe to the bathroom. I put on some clothes and sneak out of the room. The door slams shut with a loud thud, of course – I hope it didn't wake him.

The reception area that was so busy earlier is completely deserted. The fluorescent lighting on the grey marble makes for an unpleasant and hostile atmosphere. I take the steps down on the left of the reception desk.

I find the Chinese basement inexplicably shut. There is a big Chinese sign above the glass door, but no light inside. Disappointed, I go back up in the lift.

'Because no Chinese visitors,' the lift man explains.

The prostitutes decided to take the night off.

CHAPTER THREE

HOW TO MAKE A NORTH KOREAN WIN THE MARATHON

It's the day of the marathon! Last night, we were invited to view a film but nobody chose to go as we were all exhausted, and the marathon runners wanted to save their strength for today.

Most runners in our group have taken part in other marathons. The New York and London ones are routine for them; three ran in the Patagonian Marathon; and one is talking about the Marathon des Sables, the toughest in the world, which takes place in the Sahara. My new friend Hong Kong Edward did the Marathon du Médoc, where, in true Gallic style, wine is served at the pit stops. That's the thing with fellow travellers to North Korea: they are invariably interesting, if not outright eccentric. Conversation never dies, and they relish new challenges.

They all arrive at 6.45 a.m. in the main hotel hall and it's still pitch dark outside. They are wearing their diverse marathon Lycra, but this is less straightforward than it seems: exhibiting flags of countries or logos of foreign corporations is expressly verboten! They are all amateurs, and there is no boasting or bragging: it's good-natured. There is always that slight siege mentality, always the feeling, everywhere and at all times, that we may have to rely upon each other in this strange place.

I ask American minder Josh what I am supposed to do while the others are running.

'You can spend the time in the stadium watching a football game. Mr Chong will stay with you,' he reassures me. 'I am not running either.'

When I look doubtful, Josh adds: 'You won't be on your own: Anna and Victor are also not running.'

I count the hours on my fingers. If I have it correctly, I will have to sit in that stadium for at least five hours.

'Josh, may I not stay at the hotel instead? I mean, I'm not really into football. I could read my book?'

He scrutinises me in silence, unblinking, in that unnerving way of his. He takes a deep breath and says that no, it is not possible, because then one of the guides would have to stay with me in the hotel.

I stare at him, disbelieving. He looks sheepish now, like a rabbit in the headlights. I don't even bother to ask him to plead my case with the North Koreans.

So in North Korea, a minder needs to stay with you even if you just spend the morning in your hotel room. Never mind that one can't really 'escape' from the hotel compound, let alone the hotel island.

It's 7.15 a.m. and, as always, car traffic is negligible. The pavements, however, are heaving with streams of people dressed in monochrome dark clothes marching to the Rungrado 1st of May Stadium. From afar they look like centipedes. Many are in large groups, and are directed to walk in lines and rows. Mrs Kim says that they obtain tickets through their work units. The whole area is also swarming with soldiers who instruct people what to do.

The stadium is a sight to behold. From the outside it is first cousin to the round dome of a traditional parachute in full flight. Its huge sequential white arches clash with the leaden sky. From above, the stadium is said to resemble a magnolia flower. With 150,000 seats, it's the largest in the world (for comparison, Wembley can hold 90,000 and the Stade de France holds 81,000). It was built to host the Olympics, but sadly shooting down a passenger flight somewhat messed up the country's hopes of carrying the flame.

It went like this: Seoul won the battle to host the 1988 Summer Olympics. Cuban President Fidel Castro campaigned to make the Olympics a joint Korean event. The International Olympic Committee even hosted talks between the North and the South in Lausanne in 1986 to find a workable compromise. North Korean negotiators demanded parity, so that at least eleven of the twenty-three sports would be held in North Korea, and there would be a joint organising committee and joint teams, along with joint opening and closing ceremonies. North Korea had already started building three new stadiums, an Olympic village and a number of international hotels to prove that it was up to the challenge. The first sparks flew when the IOC stated that only a fraction of the events would be awarded to North Korea. And then the South

Korean Air Flight 858 exploded over the Andaman Sea (south of Myanmar), killing all 115 civilians on board.

The two North Korean agents who planted the bomb were traced to Bahrain. One took a cyanide pill. That in itself was already a giveaway: only secret services possess cyanide pills. The other bomber, a woman called Kim Hyon-hui, was arrested and extradited to South Korea, where she was sentenced to death. South Korean president Roh Tae-woo, however, pardoned her, 'because she had been brainwashed'. She became a vocal critic of North Korea and now lives in exile in South Korea with around-the-clock security protection. In her very moving book *Tears of My Soul* she describes how she was personally ordered by Kim Jong-il to carry out the outrage.

North Korea has its own version of events. They say that Kim Hyon-hui was not even born in the North, and that the whole story was a South Korean fabrication. Kim Hyon-hui was said to be an agent for the Japanese 'war criminals, the American imperialists, and the South Korean puppet regime'. North Korea says that South Korea bombed its own plane in order to blame the North for the outrage and to ensure that General Roh Tae-woo, the handpicked candidate of outgoing General Chun Doo-hwan, won the first democratic elections in South Korea. The South Korean opposition candidate Chun was supposed to be friendlier to North Korea than his opponent.* If you think about it, it is true that the pariah state did not profit from the plane bombing.

---

* General Roh Tae-woo did win the South Korean presidential elections, but mainly because the opposition vote was split between two candidates.

Whatever the truth is, the killing of 115 civilian passengers ended North Korea's ambition to co-host the 1988 Olympics. North Korea's rhetoric returned to form, and the Olympics in Seoul were denounced as 'a major triumph for its American imperialist puppet masters' and a cunning scheme 'to make the world believe that their colony was an independent state'. North Korea also called for a boycott of the Seoul games, a call that was heeded by just three of its allies: Cuba, Ethiopia and Nicaragua.

When not used for sporting events, the Rungrado Stadium serves to celebrate the Kim in charge. It is here that the mass gymnastics of the Arirang Festival take place. Tens of thousands of people hold up coloured cards so that from afar, gigantic images of hammer, sickle and paintbrush along with images of the Leader and slogans in red appear. It's a finely choreographed exercise in discipline and obliteration of the individual to achieve collective goals: precisely the 'values' the dictatorship wants to instil in the people. The Festival feels like an almost religious expression of unity between the Supreme Leader and the masses.

It is rumoured that, in the late 1990s, a number of North Korean generals who had conspired to assassinate Kim Jong-il were executed in the stadium by being doused in petrol and burned alive. I found only one source for this story. Perhaps this was one of the cunning inventions of the South Korean intelligence service who happily plant outrageous stories about North Korea in the media. Then again, the public-burning story is not entirely out of sync with the antics of the leadership. And in a country where the population is too terrorised to attempt a revolution, the possibility of a military putsch must be the main fear of the Great Leader. Generals are routinely purged to dissuade the others from making a move. There is also a raft of other measures in place to make a putsch less likely. Different army units, for example, are not allowed to communicate with each other.

Today the stadium is about half full, with only the lower tier occupied. From their portraits high above, the Great Leaders are watching us. We are herded to our seats in a block reserved for foreigners. Workers' Party of Korea badge-carriers keep their suspicious eyes on us at all times. For some reason each block also has one lady hostess in saccharine-coloured national hoop-dress.

Stately music heralds the opening ceremony. Officially, this is called the Mangyongdae Prize International Marathon.* The delegations from the different countries march into the stadium in a rather disorderly fashion. Most are waving and somehow taking selfies simultaneously. They need to be careful, as they have been officially told not to take photos of the generals who are watching. They have also been told not to take cropped photos of the Leaders' statues. It isn't clear whether these runners are organised by country or according to the different distances they will run, since the placards that are carried ahead of the different cohorts of runners are in Korean.

The runners gather in a number of large groups in the centre of the grass stadium. The loudspeakers are switched on. After a deafening microphone shriek, a woman starts to make a speech in Korean.

---

* Mangyongdae is Kim Il-sung's alleged birthplace.

She speaks in the same excited, reverential timbre always reserved for the Great Leaders Kim Il-sung, Kim Jong-il and Kim Jong-un. Whenever one or several are mentioned, the masses applaud. Then the marathon runners are lined up. Long-legged professionals flown in from an assortment of African countries have been positioned in the front.

A pistol shot is fired, and off they go! Not all though: quite a few slow down to take selfies. The football game in the centre of the stadium starts at the same time. is the race is already well on its way when some dazed runners enter the stadium. Did they oversleep? They see the disappearing derrières of the last runners at the other end and run after them, to the mocking mirth of the public. It's all very good-natured.

We, the non-participants in our group, have to vegetate in the stadium for the rest of the morning. Our American minder Josh, whose company I had been looking forward to, is busy enjoying himself somewhere else. Mrs Kim is nowhere to be seen either, so it is just poor Mr Chong as our guard today. I think he doesn't like football either as he merely drops us there, tells us not to move and then disappears as well.

The three of us are bored out of our wits. Colombian Anna complains of the cold as soon as the scorching sun disappears behind the stadium's awning. Portly Victor, an IT genius from Lithuania who does brilliant things with the stateless currency Bitcoin, complains about the small size of the seats and how they make his back hurt. He sits on three seats and the plastic backs bulge outwards. As he is hungry he leaves regularly to buy snacks and soft drinks but regrets that it's only 10 a.m. and beer is not for sale yet.

My mood is not lifted by the cacophony caused by the six or seven brass bands spread out among the audience, who all perform different tunes at top volume *at the same time*. I observe the locals and take a lot of photos. While part of the audience clap and roar when a goal is scored, the others just sit there, morose and unsmiling, as if suffering toothache. They are all dressed in dark colours, and many wear uniforms. Behind us is an entire block of a few hundred reluctant spectators who don't smile or participate in the ubiquitous clapping at all.

A Japanese spectator next to me sees me staring at them.

'They were forced to attend, to fill the stadium. That's what our guide said,' he volunteers.

Having crossed my legs for the umpteenth time and having tried every possible permutation to try to sit comfortably on the cramped seats, I decide to go outside and walk around the stadium. The edifice is so vast that it takes about fifteen minutes to do this. The North Korean civilians who meet me look at me as if I am from outer space. Even if they had been taught English in school, none will risk the concentration camp by talking to me.

I start to think about the camps. North Korea's prison camps are sometimes called 'labour camps' or 'gulags', but they ought to be called concentration camps. Their regime is extremely brutal; very large numbers of people are held there and most inmates do not leave the camps alive.

A few years ago I attended a talk in the UK Houses of Parliament by Shin Dong-hyuk, who famously escaped from a North Korean political concentration camp. He was born in Camp Number 14 in Kaechon, north of Pyongyang, as the child of prisoners. In the camp, he was subjected to torture and forced labour, and he was severely malnourished. At the age of fourteen, he saw his brother and mother being executed after they attempted to escape. He knew what the world outside was like only from talking to newly arrived inmates. He escaped in 2005 aged twenty-three by climbing over the body of his friend who had been electrocuted by one of the fences surrounding the camp. If Shin had not escaped the camp, he would have died inside it.

The North Korean dictatorship does not admit that the concentration camps exist, so what we know about the camps comes mainly from defectors. Satellite photos show how many there are and where they are located. In the 1990s it was estimated that there were between 150,000 and 200,000 inmates in political camps.* In 2013 new estimates were made, and it is now thought that there are between 80,000 and 120,000 prisoners in five camps. The reduced numbers do not mean that the regime has 'loosened up': rather, it means that many political prisoners have simply died. North Korea still has the highest number of political prisoners prorate its population in the world.

Most North Koreans are aware of the concentration camps but do not know what goes on inside. Alessandro Ford, one of the few Westerners ever to attend Kim Il-sung University, asked fellow

---

* This is about 1 per cent of the North Korean population. Transposed to Britain, that would mean 650,000 people.

students what they thought about the camps. One girl replied that they 'served to educate people who did not understand the Great Leader's thoughts' – as if they were some sort of remedial classes for slow pupils.

What sort of concentration camp you are sent to depends upon whether you are accused of a conventional or a political crime. If one is accused of a conventional crime, the North Korean Constitution and the Law of Court Procedure impose rules and certain rights. This does not mean, however, that the 'guarantees' are guaranteed. Arbitrary detention in complete disregard of the official judicial procedure is the rule rather than the exception.

For a conventional crime, you are unlikely to be presented with an arrest warrant when you are arrested. If there is an actual trial, it will be a mere formality. Judges are not independent: they are elected by the political assemblies that are controlled by the Korean Workers' Party. Prosecutors have higher authority than judges. The sentence is often decided at pre-trial stage, without juries and judge having any say in it. During the trial, you will not be allowed to speak. A defence lawyer will be allocated to you, but lawyers are not independent and their main task is to make you confess. You *will* be found guilty.

Sometimes detainees are carted off to a camp without trial, without being heard, and with no legal representation. A court will simply issue a written decision.

The trial may be held on-site to instil terror in the public; for example on the factory floor, or in the main square in a village. What types of crimes are heard on-site depends upon which crimes are bugging the Korean Workers' Party at that time. Sometimes this is followed by a public execution by firing squad. On occasion, when all members of a group are accused of the same crime, only one is executed. It is then announced that Kim Jong-un is giving the others a second chance. The pardoned will thank the Leader in tears. This does not mean that they are released: they may still be carted off for a fixed term to a camp.

The camps for conventional crimes are run by the police. Petty thieves, those caught crossing the border for smuggling or those who sin against public morality – such as women who wear skinny jeans – will be sent to a labour training camp. Half the day is spent doing forced labour and the other half is spent in re-education. Security is lax, and escapes do occur. More serious criminals, such as murderers or even those who smuggled DVDs across the border, are sent to re-education camps. The regime is tough in these camps: fourteen hours' forced labour in a salt mine without safety measures is normal. Food provision is insufficient.

Political crimes are dealt with in a completely different way. These include watching a South Korean video, saying something favourable about South Korea, the defection of a family member, attending a church service, making a phone call to someone in the south etc.

For political crimes, North Korea applies its 'guilt by association' system. Not only the accused but also the family members up to three generations removed will be punished. This *Yeonjwaje-*system was already practised in Korea's past. This collective punishment is probably the main reason why the Kim dynasty has not been toppled yet by a popular uprising. You may be willing to risk your own life for your own political beliefs, but what if your parents, grandparents, wife, children, grandchildren, brothers and sisters are dragged to the concentration camp as well?*

How are 'political crimes' detected? It is estimated that there is about one informer per fifty citizens. There will be informers in your neighbourhood (*inminban*), your place of work and the associations you are obliged to be a member of. *Inminban* leaders know everything about you and even possess the keys of your home.

The investigation, trial and the camps themselves are run by the State Security Department. The SSD is not subject to the law, the courts or due process. If the SSD has decided to arrest you, you are lost.

You will either be picked up without warning or you will be told to appear somewhere on a specific day.** They may pick you up from the street or your place of work, or you and your family may be shoved into a lorry in the middle of the night. Nobody will be notified of your arrest, the reason behind it or the location of your detention. You will not be presented with an arrest warrant. If you are lucky you may be given one hour to pack your belongings.

The State Security Department's prosecutor will make a final decision about your guilt and your sentence, and about which members of your family will also be sent to the camp. There is no

---

* According to defectors, it is usually only the immediate blood family who are co-punished under the system. The wife or husband may escape by divorcing the other.
** Being asked to appear somewhere at a given time is seen as merciful as it allows you to commit suicide. This would solve the problem only for yourself though: people who take their own lives are labelled traitors, and surviving family members risk punishment.

appeal. You will then be taken away, your property confiscated and your home re-allocated.

Alternatively, you can be lucky in two ways. Instead of ending up in a concentration camp, you may just be sent into internal exile; to describe this, North Koreans say that somebody 'has gone to the mountains'. Or you may be sent to a non-political prison instead. The system is so opaque and completely at the whim of the SSD that it is impossible to tell why some are so favoured.

Camps for political prisoners, called *kwanliso*, are much more brutal than camps for conventional crimes. Kim Il-sung copied them from Stalin in the 1950s. It is likely that you will die in the camp. You will have no contact with the outside. In fact, outsiders will often not know that you are in a camp.

There are two different control regimes inside the political camps: there is a Revolutionising Zone and there is a Zone of Absolute Control. If, for example, you watched South Korean TV, you may be sent to a Revolutionising Zone. Usually family members are sent to the former, and the actual 'culprit' to the latter. The Revolutionising Zone allows family members to stay together, work and walk free inside the zone. One can even have children. You will, however, have to sit through many indoctrination classes, as well as self-criticism sessions where you have to confess your misdeeds in front of other prisoners who are encouraged to condemn your behaviour and add more criticism of their own. If your evaluation shows that you have been re-educated, you may be released. Before you are released, you must sign an oath that you will not divulge information about life inside the camp, and if you break your oath you will be sent back. After your release, you will be labelled 'hostile class', put under surveillance by the security service, and your daily activities such as work and travel will be restricted.

One is not supposed to leave an Absolute Control Zone alive.* The sentence is lifetime confinement with no chance of release. One becomes a non-person who deserves death but who, through the mercy of the state, is allowed to carry out hard labour till death instead. Inmates die due to underfeeding, atrocious living conditions, lack of medical care and backbreaking work. In fact, not even dead bodies leave the Absolute Control Zones: they are burned.

Unlike other former socialist countries, North Korean psychiatric institutions are not used to getting rid of political dissidents. The concentration camps solve the regime's problems.

When I come back from my little constitutional around the stadium, a terrified-looking Mr Chong grabs me harshly by the arm and guides me back to my seat. My minder feared he had lost me.

---

* In an Absolute Control Zone, the most severe of the two kinds of concentration camps, the gaolers don't even bother with indoctrination lessons any more: you are deemed beyond redemption. You will carry out hard labour all day, probably in a mine, farming or logging. The management maximises the workload to attain the camp's production quota. In a coal mine, for example, you will have your own daily production quota and if that is not met, you simply continue working till it is. There are no days off. You will receive insufficient food, and no medical treatment. When you are too ill to work you will be brought to a sanatorium for critical patients. As there are usually no medicines or doctors available, you will be left to die. One defector testified how in April 2004 in the Yongjong Hospital in the concentration camp of Buckang, medical staff took one X-ray of his injured leg, and then told him his leg should be amputated. Forced abortions are routine. At night one is cooped up in overcrowded and insanitary barracks. Some turn to cannibalism. At all times one is subject to extreme brutality. The way to survive is by being completely submissive and never to ask questions. Some people don't know why they are in the concentration camp in the first place. If they are so silly to ask, they are shot. The SSD expressly employs psychopaths to guard and run Zones of Absolute Control. It is unclear whether family members are released when a person dies in a Zone of Absolute Control.

Would he have been fired, or been sent to a concentration camp? I decide to give him a few more frights, just for the sport of it.

After two hours, the runners start to arrive back. I bump into Matt, my friend from London who had asked me to come to Pyongyang to run the marathon. In the end I did not travel with his group as I wanted to stay for longer than the three-day sightseeing trip he was on. He tells me how the running went. Scores of men, women and children massed the roads, happily cheering, high-fiving and shouting to run faster. But as soon as one raised a camera, they scattered! There were plenty of guards along the route as well. Matt deliberately smiled and said hello to an ashen-faced general at 8km. The general scowled, unlike the happy people around him. During the run, Matt's playlist included such songs as 'I Want to Break Free', 'Living in America' and 'Rule Britannia'.

Several runners, who are just arriving, breathlessly report an extraordinary story. Foreigners would obviously be unfamiliar with the marathon route, and so those running in the front were told to follow a white van. A few hundred metres before the finishing line, the Ethiopian runner Ketema Bekele Negasa was ahead of North Korean Pak Chol. Suddenly, the van swerved to the left, and Ketema followed it as instructed. Pak Chol kept running straight. When Ketema realised that something was amiss, he quickly went after Pak Chol. But by then it was too late and Pak Chol won the race. The 80,000 North Koreans in the stadium were ecstatic. Is this what happened? In the media I find nothing about this. Clearly, a tyranny doesn't necessarily need state-sponsored doping programmes to make sure its athletes are victorious.

Inside the stadium, the second football game is still going strong. This is followed by the closing ceremony, which I can't be bothered to attend. I just lie outside on the grass, taking in the hard-hitting sun and watching the world go by. I wonder what the reason could be for one of the poorest countries in the world to have the largest stadium. Again and again over the next few days, we see large public buildings and institutions that are disproportionate to the size and global standing of North Korea. Attendance at the public events venues is more or less compulsory. The regime likes to distract the population with games, since a football game or a festival is always better than people having spare time to think (and talk!) about hunger, tyranny and lack of freedom. Rome's *panem et circenses* are alive and kicking in the DPRK. Well, without the *panem*, that is.

After we wait for an eternity for those who ran the marathon to finish, we are split into two groups. One part will attend the Pyongyang water park, and the others will go on a city trip. Several exhausted marathon runners opt for the water park; I opt for the city trip. At the entrance of the water park, the others are apparently welcomed by a wax model of a beaming Kim Jong-il in army-green shell suit. He is standing in front of a photo of a beach with a Caribbean sea and colourful beach umbrellas. The guide warns them not to laugh at the waxwork. They all burst into laughter as soon as they have safely boarded the coach.

One side-effect of the group-splitting is that the unpleasant set of minders from the other group joins ours. This includes their boorish and fanatical Gruppenführerin who, in just three days' time, has managed to build up a very negative reputation among us foreigners. She regularly asks to see the photos on our cameras and deletes what she deems inadmissible. She is about five foot tall and has a plain, round, acne-ridden face.

Our first stop is the 170m Juche Tower. It's built out of 25,550 granite blocks: one for each day of Kim Il-sung's life. The phallic tower is capped with a 20m-high illuminated torch. Our guide excitedly tells us that it surpasses the Washington Monument by 1m.

Kim Il-sung had it built in 1982 to celebrate his seventieth birthday. It is dedicated to Juche, the official state ideology of this pariah state.

Juche was introduced by Kim Il-sung. He first referred to it in a speech in 1955 to underpin a political purge of 'impure' individuals. Kim concocted his own ideology to pose as a philosophical giant like Marx, Engels and Lenin. It was similar to Mao's slightly earlier creation of Maoism, the particularly vicious brand of communism. Kim was eager to shed China's and the Soviet Union's tutelage, and Juche was said to be distinct from ordinary communism; and much superior to it, as it was uniquely adapted to Korean history and society. The last portrait of Marx in Pyongyang was removed in 2012 when Kim Jong-un came to power. In *Nineteen Eighty-Four* Juche would have been called Insoc: an ideology based on socialism, but where the totalitarian government tries to obscure the origins as it is constantly rewriting history.

The word Juche means self-reliance (autarky). It's a hotchpotch of communism, nationalism, Stalinism, racism and Confucianism. The Juche state is not only based on traditional communist principles such as the state ownership of the means of production, the command economy and the total absence of private owner-ship, it also strives to make that state economically, militarily and politically self-reliant.

According to Juche, man is master of his own destiny. He can steer society in whatever direction he decides. Juche therefore rejects materialism or determinism. In an irrational twist, 'man being master of his own destiny' somehow does *not* mean that the individuals living under Juche ideology are masters of their own destiny. Only the Great Leader represents the masses. The working classes are not to think for themselves; that is the Great Leader's job. The dictatorship of the mind is total. Making a mistake is not doing as you have been told by the Leader.* The Great Leader never makes mistakes and he rules for the public good. He is incorrupti-ble. Without its Leader, the masses cannot survive. Obedience to authority, knowing one's place, and the father–son relationship all seem to come from traditional Confucianism. The idea of dynastic succession was added to the theory by crown prince Kim Jong-il in the 1970s.

The self-reliance obsession legitimises cutting off the popula-tion from all outside influences or contacts. As such it is a means to keep the Kims firmly in power.

The Kims portray Juche as an ideology superior to all others. They say that other communist countries collapsed because they

---

* Three generations of Kims have been alleged geniuses in all aspects of human endeavour. Wher-ever they turn up, they give on-the-spot guidance, e.g. telling farmers how to increase their crop yield.

had too slavishly adopted the policies of the Soviet Union.* Juche is said to be different because it is uniquely adapted to Korea and to the Korean race. This fervent nationalism has caused some to say that North Korea is a national-socialist, rather than a socialist state. It is true that the regime thrives on denunciations of foreigners and foreign states and that it prides itself on being mono-cultural. However, a socialist command economy is the core element of North Korea's system.

From an economic point of view, any country's drive towards self-reliance makes no sense whatsoever. Trying to create products in order to be self-reliant, even when your climate/work-force/circumstances/natural resources are not suitable, creates a huge economic cost. It makes no sense to try to make red wine in Antarctica. It causes an inefficient misallocation of labour, machines and capital towards political, instead of demand-driven economic goals.

This high cost of self-reliance, together with the traditional socialist absence of market price signals, the profit motive and protection of private property, are the reasons why North Korea not only fails like all other socialist states, but fails exponentially. It is as if cholera is added to plague.** During the thirty-five years they occupied Korea, the Japanese industrialised the north and

---

* Initially, North Koreans were kept completely in the dark when popular revolutions swept away the communist regimes in Eastern Europe.
** Historically, forms of autarky were attempted by the great Empires of Europe under the system of 'Mercantilism'. When the industrial revolution proved that an open economy creates far greater wealth, mercantilism was swept away. Nazi Germany attempted to return to it and one of the reasons it lost the war was that, because of centralised misallocation of resources, by the end of the war it had massive shortages of everything.

kept the south agricultural. So, when the communists took over North Korea in 1945, they began with a substantial economic advantage compared with South Korea. After seventy-two years of communism in the north and capitalism in the south, North Korea has a GDP of $25 billion and South Korea of $1.4 trillion.

'Juche is the philosophy of slavery,' New Zealand James says while we walk up to the Juche Tower. 'People are made subject to the Leader, who decides everything. People risk their lives and limbs if they disobey. When the economy finally collapsed in the 1990s, people's salaries were no longer paid, but they still had to turn up for work. They are, therefore, slaves.'

I don't reply.

Inside the Juche Tower, a wall with plaques of Juche societies in eighty-five countries serves to prove that the ideology has international appeal. Most groups suggest tiny membership and great obscurity, if they exist at all. My suspicion grows that 'Juche Idea Study Group, England' has been made up. Later, when I am back in the UK, I do indeed find a 'Juche Idea Study Group of England' on Facebook. Reading their Facebook page,* it occurs to me that this group would not be out of place in an entire volume dedicated to English eccentrics.

---

* 719 People 'Liked' the Juche Idea Study Group of England on Facebook. The page offers some useful information: they were formed in 1985 in Winchester as 'the Group for the Study of Marshal Kim Il Sung's Works'. They 'reformed the group in 1990 and renamed the group in 1995 to incorporate the name of the illustrious General Kim Jong Il into (their) title'. Activities include study meetings, seminars and participating in events organised by the Society of Friendship with Korea. They have members in London, Stoke-on-Trent and 'other areas'. It is open to those who support the Juche Idea wholeheartedly; want to apply the Juche Idea in England; and support the DPRK, the Workers' Party of Korea, and the Great Leaders comrade Kim Il-sung and Kim Jong-il.

Up in the lift we go, with a woman in long, black velvet robe with diamanté sequins and the regulation socialist perm, who is gainfully employed to push the up and down buttons. Up high, both the view and the wind are breath-taking. Downtown Pyongyang lies at our feet. The Juche Tower is on an axis with Kim Il-sung Square and with the Grand Study House. The afternoon light is Naples-yellow, golden and extremely beautiful. We walk around the viewing platform and take panoramic photos. On one side we see the residential housing estates: straight modernist blocks painted in pastel colours. It is striking how neatly lined up and clean everything looks. In poverty-stricken and therefore transport-poor North Korea, there does not appear to be any smog. The wind whistles as it rushes around the tower. To avert frostbite I quickly snap away, and then hurry back into the lift.

Terraces lead to the river bank, which is basking in the golden light. Large sculptures represent 'Bumper Harvests', 'Juche Art', 'The Land of Learning', 'Longevity' and 'Impregnable Fortress'. I obtain special permission from American minder Josh to photograph the rather pretty pagoda-style annexe about 50m away, but am thwarted in my attempts as soldiers are camping behind it, and I remember the edict not to photograph soldiers. So I return empty-handed to a now-terrified Josh. He is not quite Colditz-escape material! A member of the other group is severely berated by the *Gruppenführerin* for accidentally leaving a newspaper featuring Kim Il-sung on a bench. Not sure whether she slapped his ear, too.

Close to the Juche Tower is the Workers' Party of Korea Foundation Monument. The Workers' Party's main task is to impose the Juche ideology on the population. Here too, an official minder is already waiting: carefully coiffed and dressed again in a floor-length black velvet robe with diamanté sequins. We stand under a massive marble-plated monument featuring a hammer, a sickle and a paintbrush. These refer to the workers, the farmers and the intellectuals: the three classes of people that the Workers' Party of Korea claims to unite. Awed by her own information, our minder explains that the intellectuals were added to the workers and the farmers to distinguish the Korean Workers' Party from other communist parties to create their own unique Korean variety. She drones on about the rather boring size stats and provides an explanation of the different bronze reliefs in the heroic workers' style. Behind the monument are two flag-shaped red apartment blocks with Korean letters, saying 'Ever Victorious'.

We stroll to another bookshop behind the monument that sells exactly the same Kim Il-sung page-turners and mud-coloured pottery as the other shops. Adjoining the bookshop is the Pyongyang Culture Exhibition Hall. The brightly lit gallery sells the writings of the Kims and mud-coloured pottery, and exhibits gaudy landscapes and photos of foreign delegations paying homage to the Kims. This includes a photo of an important delegation from the European Union, headed by none other than a bemused looking Chris Patten! Unfortunately, taking photos of these propaganda photos is not allowed.

Just before we mount the coach, a group of women in traditional dress arrive to dance on a square. The sun is setting. Once again, we are struck by the candy-shop colours and whimsical form of the hoop-dresses – as if the grown women of this country have been turned into children's fairy-tale dolls. When they switch on the cassette tape and start dancing on the concrete slabs we are urgently commanded by the *Gruppenführerin* to 'photograph monument, not people!' Matt's group yesterday was allowed to dance with the locals (it was clear that their arty renditions did not endanger them from being invited to become permanent members of the dance group). Our *Gruppenführerin* is not putting up with such loose behaviour.

Dinner at the hotel is ghastly. There is less food than before, but it is even blander. The state must have decided that high-calorie grub is no longer a priority now that most marathon runners have left.

My friend Matt says that the hotel room TV gives access to BBC World, and so it does when I try it later. Back in the UK some Labour Party shadow minister has asked for the resignation of Prime Minister David Cameron because Cameron's father was mentioned in the leaked Panama Papers that disclosed international tax evasion schemes set up by the law firm Mossack Fonseca. I don't think the BBC World edition would have been viewable here in Pyongyang if it had discussed Fonseca's part in setting up the offshore company DCB Finance. DCB Finance's owners and directors were based in Pyongyang, and the company was linked to a bank that is used to fund North Korea's nuclear weapons programme and arms sales. Fonseca allegedly continued to act for this company even after it was blacklisted by the US Treasury.

It is illegal for North Koreans to tune into foreign TV channels and watching or distributing South Korean films is punishable by death. When you buy a TV set in North Korea it is pre-tuned to North Korean stations only. The Wave Inspection Bureau sets it to the government's stations and seals the tuners. This prevents reception of any outside information, but the seals can be broken or tampered with. Inspectors pay surprise home inspection visits to check the seals.

Previously, few North Koreans risked being sent to the concentration camp, but since the economic crisis, most officials can be bribed – so in border regions where foreign stations can be received, North Koreans routinely watch Chinese and South Korean TV.

Some North Koreans have smuggled in cheap DVD players from China to watch South Korean soaps and US films. Smugglers can easily bring over 1,000 pirated DVDs per trip. DVDs will cost about one dollar in the market; one simply has to ask the trader whether they have 'something special' for sale. Again, there is the on-going threat of inspection. A typical trick the inspectors use is to turn the electricity in an apartment block off, and then raid the flats with the foreign DVDs still stuck in the player. Often the inspectors are bribed or watch the films themselves. Defectors have given evidence that they witnessed public executions for those 'crimes'. In fact, it is believed that the death sentence is on the increase for this. A more recent trend is to watch films or information on USB sticks.

North Koreans will have sat through countless Workers' Party lectures telling them that the CIA doctors films to make the capitalist world look more attractive. Still, the images grab the attention:

the viewers see the household appliances and the many cars in the background of South Korean soaps. As a result, the government's tale that South Koreans are poor and suffering is no longer believed by ordinary North Koreans.

Sadly, few DVDs cover life in North Korea. Perhaps this is why the American slapstick comedy *The Interview* was attacked with such vehemence by the dictatorship. It was met with sheer fear that North Koreans would see it. The synopsis goes thus: two American journalists are invited to North Korea to interview Kim Jong-un and the CIA recruits them to kill the Great Leader. This leads to a number of highly comical situations. The scary thing is, however, that so many of the images are utterly recognisable to anyone who has visited North Korea. North Korea threatened action against the United States if the film was released, calling it a 'most blatant act of terrorism and war' because (spoiler-alert!) Kim is assassinated in the film. Columbia Pictures delayed the release and edited the film to make it more acceptable. They, for example, reduced the screen-time of Kim's death scene. But to no avail: Sony, the parent company, was hacked by the 'Guardians of Peace', a group linked to North Korea. The group threatened to attack cinemas that showed the film. But after a few showings in select cinemas, Sony released it for online rental and purchase only, and it became clear that the North Korean dictatorship's outburst had worked wonders: *The Interview* grossed $40 million in digital rental, Sony's highest-grossing rental release ever. North Korean resistance organisations based in South Korea promised to export the DVDs in huge numbers to North Korea.

North Korean news broadcasts are hilarious to listen to. An excited wavering voice is used whenever the Leaders are praised; and a hateful one whenever a hostile foreign country* is denounced (i.e. most countries). The news broadcasts typically include riveting exposés about bumper harvests, industrial production targets having been exceeded, natural disasters or strikes in capitalist countries and interviews with small groups in obscure African countries studying Juche thought. The night before national holidays, e.g. to celebrate the birthdays of the Kims, state media broadcasts endless footage hailing the heroic deeds of the Leaders. It's forbidden to talk or fall asleep during the broadcasts.

In a poor country like North Korea, most news is obtained from radio broadcasts. Just as with television sets, radios bought in North Korea are pre-set to North Korean stations. It is illegal to listen to foreign stations and foreign radio sets are sealed. Again, while clever cookies can easily 'fix' this, inspectors or the head of the *inminban* can enter your home and check the seal at all times. Some daredevils simply buy a second radio set or bribe the inspector. Many officials see illegal radio ownership as a never-ending source of bribes.

There are about forty-five stations to listen to in North Korea, including a 'black propaganda' station set up by the regime purporting to broadcast from South Korea. Some foreign broadcast programmes aimed at North Korea are jammed by the dictatorship

---

* Particularly America, Israel, South Korea, China, the United Nations – or, after they entered into diplomatic relations with the 'puppet regime' in South Korea, even former allies like Russia, Hungary or Poland.

by way of jet-plane noise. There exists a Free North Korea Station that beams out information from South Korea on how to escape from the country. Programmes by defectors are particularly appreciated by North Korean listeners.

But what may ultimately prove to be the undoing of North Korean media censorship is simple fashion. For North Korean youths, North Korean soaps, television, radio and music are seriously 'uncool'.

I spend the rest of the evening in drunken revelry with Matt in a small booth in the hotel bar, which features a Christmas tree (it's May). The bar is divided from the main hall by way of a large aquarium where fish try to find their way around in a grey soup. Will they be prepared in the kitchen when fully mature? Or when they die from asphyxiation in their insalubrious tank?

'Are you excited about our outing tomorrow?' Matt asks.

'I haven't heard. Where are we off to?'

'Tomorrow, we are going to pay our respect to the Leaders' statues,' Matt replies. 'Brace yourself. And make sure there is not photographic evidence.'

CHAPTER FOUR

BOWING TO THE TYRANTS' STATUES

When I spot Mrs Kim in the reception hall of the hotel that morning, I am again taken aback by how well-dressed she is.

'I made it myself,' her surprising reply comes.

'How so?'

'It's my hobby. I like designing clothes. I mean: I do not cut and sew them myself; I go to a tailor and tell her how to do it.'

'Wow. It's exquisite. Could have come straight from Paris.'

Does she associate Paris with fashion? Her eyes sparkle. She looks exceedingly pleased. She knows.

'Would you not rather be a fashion designer than a tour guide?'

She sighs. 'I would, but it's too late. I would need to give up my job and go study again for many years.'

We say nothing for a few moments. In North Korea, the state allocates jobs to individuals, irrespective of the individuals' personal desires or views. The authorities simply decide that '600 people are needed for the Gougeon Won Coal Mine', and 600 are duly found and sent off.

Officially, there is no unemployment. Everybody is allocated a job, but if it pays a salary at all, it is rarely sufficient to live off. Working is not just a right, but also a duty. If you don't turn up, even when your pay arrives six months late or not at all, you will be punished. There are no employment contracts. To transfer to a different job, you need official approval. How would Mrs Kim explain to the official that she wants a break from her well-paid tourist guide job to study fashion design? I can't imagine there being a huge market in North Korea for Parisian fineries anyway. If they were liberated, on the other hand … I almost tell her to play the long game.

'So do you have all your clothes made by a tailor?'

'Oh, no. Some things I just buy. Sometimes North Korean-made, and sometimes from abroad. From abroad is much more expensive.'

'And what is that?' I ask, pointing at the little square badge with the juxtaposed images of Kim Il-sung and Kim Jong-un pinned on her left shoulder. I have noticed that most people sport one.

'It is a pin to show that we are patriots,' she says, and turns to others from the group who have just arrived.

The Workers' Party of Korea started to distribute these lapel pins on the occasion of Kim Il-sung's sixtieth birthday in 1972. Soon they were compulsory. They have to be worn on the left breast (on the heart). Usually it's Kim Il-sung alone who is portrayed. There are many varieties of badges, which tell you a great deal about the wearer. Officials sport a very exclusive one. And what does it say about the rare individuals who do not put one on? My mind drifts off to Nazi Party pins, some of which were made of gold.

The Mansudae Fountain Park in the heart of Pyongyang was opened in 1976. It's located on the Mansu Hill, right behind the Grand Study House with its pagoda-style roof. It consists of paving slabs and concrete ponds with fountains and decorative rocks. One jet of water spouts 80m high. Another fountain consists of a sort of metal afro on a stick that exhales a fine mist. In the middle stands a large concrete statue of women performing a dance called 'snow falls'. Are they dancing for Kim Il-sung, who dedicated this park to his own glory? In the sun and set off against the bluest sky, the statues look so white that they could have been painted five minutes ago.

'This is a romantic spot,' Mrs Kim explains, searching in vain for our enthusiasm. 'This park is often used to take wedding photos.'

I look around. Small groups of boys and girls sit on the benches and the grass, but the sexes are strictly separated. If this is a romantic spot, perhaps the action takes place after dark? North Korea is notoriously prudish. Even holding hands in daylight is seen as an affront to public morality.

We buy flowers from an 'impromptu' flower seller, pre-approved for us by the state travel agency, at a whopping five dollars a bunch. We will have to deposit these flowers at the feet of the Great Leaders' statues. The flower selling must be some sort of private business. Perhaps our minders or the travel agency receive a cut? Like many companies that are nominally owned by the state, some of the travel agencies are in fact privately run, and compete with each other.

We are given an etiquette lesson before approaching the Mansu-dae Grand Monument:

'No joking or running. No arms crossing. No flip-flops,' Mrs Kim orders.

'Erm?' English Dan says, looking down at his shorts.

Mrs Kim stares harshly at them for several seconds.

'Shorts will be fine.' Her lips stay pursed. Dan looks sheepish.

'We will bow in group, lay flowers, and only then you can take photos. Make sure that the photo is of the entire statue, not just part of it; taking a partial photo is disrespectful. Please do not take photos from behind the statues, or of their feet. Please do not try to be 'cute' in the photo, like posing or something. And please do not keep your hands in your pockets: show respect.'

I am apprehensive. Fact is that I knew well in advance that the bowing in front of the statues was part of the deal. I will have to hold my nose.

The statues of Kim Il-sung and Kim Jong-il are 22m high: the highest ones in the country. Now a gaudy, coppery bronze, Kim Il-sung's used to be covered in gold leaf. It was removed when a bigwig from China passed by and acerbically observed that if North Korea had golden statues it obviously did not need Chinese aid.

Kim Il-sung is portrayed with tie and overcoat. Kim Jong-il, in characteristic shell suit and anorak, was added after he died in 2011. Uriminsokkiri, a website run by North Korea's Central News

Agency, once reported that Kim's shell suit had become fashionable the world over. The present Leader, Kim Jong-un, usually wears Mao suits – Pyongyangologists believe they are made of Savile Row cloth. At the same time as his son's statue was added, Kim Il-sung's previous stern face was given a make-over and turned into a smiling one.

'Will Kim III later be added too?' our trouble-making Lithuanian asks.

Mrs Kim doesn't hear the question.

The shiny gods look out over another square the size of several football pitches, with far-reaching views over Pyongyang. Left and right of the square stand more than 200 sculptures 5m high, in the heroic workers' style. They portray the wars against the Japanese and the United States, and feature machine guns and assault weapons delicately hewn in granite. Behind the Leaders is a mosaic depiction of Paektu Mountain, the mythological birthplace of the Korean people. North Korean's invented history alleges that Kim Jong-il was miraculously born in a log cabin in a secret military camp on that same mountain. This is a bit peculiar, as there is evidence that, at the time, the Kims' household was in fact in the village of Vyatskoye, near Khabarovsk in the Soviet Union. Perhaps they used a Star Trek-type transporter? To cover up that little inconvenient fact of his diverging whereabouts, Kim's year of birth has been 'amended' from 1941 to 1942. According to state propaganda, a double rainbow appeared and spring broke out simultaneously when Kim was born.

Now the bowing to the statues will take place. Our uninvited camera man is annoyingly present. He will film our entire trip, though Josh has warned that it is likely to feature not just what we saw, but also what we missed. Kim Kubrick will charge fifty euros for his DVD production.

As a budding politician, I do not want my bowing to the tyrants' statues recorded. For a second I consider asking Kim Kubrick not to film us at all. Perhaps filming is disrespectful, just like taking photos *before* the bowing has taken place?

At the crucial moment, seconds before the bowing, I take one step back ... and disappear behind the tall Lithuanian next to me. Presto: I will not feature in this North Korean blockbuster. At different times during the trip we see footage of bowing and clapping foreigners being used in routine propaganda films to prove the planetary appeal of the Supreme Leaders.

With straight faces, we stand in line at the feet of the Great Leaders and bow. We demurely fold into two until our minders stand up straight again.

The ceremony is not over yet. We now lay the flowers on the marble ledge at the feet of the Great Leaders. We do this with some trepidation, as there are already other bouquets there: are we allowed to stack them, or is that disrespectful?

Thoughts of freedom are dashed when Mrs Kim has the bright idea that this would be quite the spot for a group photo. I quickly take the same evasive action as earlier and the end product features only my left cheek and one eye, much to the mirth of my uncomprehending co-passengers when we are shown the photo a few days later.

When we walk back to the coach, a group of about fifty women in pastel-coloured hoop-gowns walk past us. We all happily snap away illicit photos.

'They go to the statues of the Great Leaders to pay their respect. All North Koreans do this on the National Holidays.'

Yeah, and if they don't, it ends up in their file.

Some North Korean couples even get married in front of the Kims' statues. In 1971, Kim Il-sung issued a rule that men should marry at thirty and women at twenty-eight.

Back on the coach, I'm absorbed about what just took place. Bowing to statues? Offering flowers to dead tyrants? It reminds me of how the Balinese offer flowers to their house gods every day.

'Mrs Kim, are these the only statues? Or are there others?'

'Oh yes,' she says. 'Every town has statues of the Great Leaders. There are more than 40,000 in total.'

'North Korea actually exports statues of leaders worldwide,' Peter, who sits next to me, whispers. 'The customers are mainly African despots. Senegalese President Abdoulaye Wade had his statue redone because when it came off the boat, it had Asian eyes.'

I express my amazement.

'Yes, statues for Africa and cheap missiles for the Middle East are North Korea's main export products.'

We snigger uncomfortably.

'Maybe we'll see them being made. They are done at the Mansudae Art Studios where we are going later today; 4,000 people work at producing statues.' Mrs Kim continues: 'Some villages are too small to have a statue. They then may have a mural with depictions of the Great Leaders instead. Also, there are obelisks, about 3,200, to celebrate Kim Il-sung. We call them "Towers of Eternal Life".

'But don't you find it strange to bow for statues and obelisks?' I ask.

She thinks about this for one moment. Then she replies: 'You have Jesus Christ, we have Kim Il-sung!'

It doesn't end with the statues. North Koreans are obliged by law to exhibit photos of the Leaders in every office, meeting hall, classroom, and even in their homes. Everywhere you go the Great Leaders are watching you. Initially, only Kim Il-sung's portrait was required; then Kim Jong-il's portrait became compulsory, too. All schools have a special 'Kim Il-sung Room' or 'Kim Jong-il Research Centre' where the photos of the Leaders and other Kim memorabilia are exhibited; for example, maquettes of the Kims' alleged birthplaces (the Mangyongdae farmhouse and the log cabin on Paektu Mountain). Pupils have to take off their shoes before going in. 'Disrespectful behaviour' such as giggling is punished. Deep bowing to the portraits is part of the proceedings.

The home portraits are provided by the state. By law, they need to be hung on a blank wall. Not even family portraits are allowed next to them – why do you need family if you have the Kims? The portraits must hang at an angle (not flat), so they can easily be seen by all people in the room. They must be hung high, because looking down on the gods' likenesses would be disrespectful. They must be cleaned every day with a cloth provided by the state, which cannot be used for anything else. The Public Standards Police used to fine the households where it found dust on the portraits during their monthly inspection. During ideological indoctrination sessions, people are told that the portraits are their most prized possessions and need to be preserved at any cost. Any damage is investigated and the culprits punished. There was a famous story, often repeated, of floods in Gangwon and South Hwanghae provinces, where the people chose to save the Kims' portraits instead of anything else. One person let his little girl be carried away by the flood because he chose to save the portrait instead. Citizens are told to emulate such heroism.

One does wonder whether these heroic stories and characters are made up by the regime; just as in *Nineteen Eighty-Four*, wherein Comrade Ogilvy, a party member, was invented by the state. Ogilvy 'showed heroism by jumping into the sea from a helicopter so his secret papers wouldn't fall into enemy hands'. North Korea beats fiction hands down, every time.

But how are the Portrait Rules enforced? The more activist heads of the *inminban* make this their business. The *inminban*, literally 'People's Group', is the neighbourhood watch which ensures that people follow the dictators' rules.

Every North Korean is a member of an *inminban*. An *inminban* usually encompasses about thirty households, e.g. a block of houses, or all the flats giving out onto a common staircase. The members are forced to carry out works such as cleaning the toilets, repairing the roads, tidying up the neighbourhood, and even going to the countryside to work in the fields. They take turns to act as security guards for their building complex. They note all the people coming in and going out in a special register.

The head of the *inminban*, the *inminbanjang*, usually an elderly woman or a retired worker, receives a state salary and greater food rations. *Inminbanjangs* are allocated a contact police officer with whom they meet regularly. They have to monitor criminal activity and political dissent. In fact, the *inminbanjang* is tasked with knowing everything about her charges, including income and spending patterns. Every evening this salaried nosy-parker must write the names of every outsider spending the night under one of her charge's roof in the register. The head of the household has the duty to report this to her. She will check their ID and, if they come from another county, their travel permit. Occasionally she and the police will organise night-time raids to catch disobedient charges. They also keep an eye on the residents' regular attendance at the statues.

It has often been argued that North Korea – with the total submission to the Leader, the veneration of the Leader's images, the Leader's absolute power and the supernatural phenomena linked to the Leader – is no longer a secular government, but a theocracy. The state ideology of Juche Thought legitimises this theocracy. The North Korean dictatorship galvanises the power of faith to achieve greater obedience from the people. In fact, one of the reasons why the regime is so averse to religion is that it fears the competition.

The deification of Kim Il-sung is formally set out in the Ten Principles for Unitary Ideology, which was created in 1974.* It imposes complete submission to the Leader and to the Workers'

---

* For the full text, see the Annexe in the back of this book.

Party. Article 3, for example, states that 'Everyone must safeguard to death and accept as absolute the authority of Great Comrade Kim Il-sung and Comrade Kim Jong-il, as well as the Party's authority.' Tell people from cradle to grave for seventy years that the Leader is infallible, like God; don't allow them any outside information; don't allow any free speech; talk incessantly of the great wisdom of the Leader; falsify history and presto: more and more people will believe that the Great Leader is God.

North Korea's state philosophy has other commonalities with organised religion in the Western world. Whenever the Leader is born, dies or does a great deed, supernatural phenomena are ascribed to it. Fantastical achievements are attributed to the Leaders: such as Kim Jong-il being able to walk and talk before he was six months old; that he won yachting races from the age of nine; and that he mastered driving a car from the age of three.

When Kim Jong-il visited a school in 1945 and smeared black paint on a school map featuring Japan, 'black clouds gathered over Japan, and heavy rain poured down'. When Kim Il-sung visited the Demilitarized Zone, 'a magical fog descended, which hid the Great Leader from snipers'. When Kim Il-sung died, 'the birds cried and a double rainbow rose over Paektu Mountain'. Kim Jong-il's birth was heralded by a star in the sky, and 'a swallow descended from heaven to announce the birth of a general who was going to rule the world'. When Kim Jong-il died, the state news agency KCNA reported that 'ice cracked on the famous Chon Lake on Paektu Mountain so loudly that is seemed to shake the Heavens and the

Earth.' In addition, 'a snowstorm waged around Mount Paektu' and 'a mysterious glow was seen'.

Then there is the quasi-religious Arirang Festival. It takes place in the May Day Stadium, where the marathon had taken place the previous day. The mass gymnastics of the opening ceremony are used to emphasise the submission of the people to their Leader. Kim Il-sung is thereby represented as their 'Father', just as in Christianity God is called 'God the Father'. Children are chosen to take part in the Arirang Festival from the age of five, a bit like First Communion in Christianity. Those chosen for the Arirang Festival, however, will then participate in it until death.

Just as in religion, North Korea is strong on iconography: the rising sun symbolises Kim Il-sung; a gun symbolises the gun Kim Il-sung gave to his son Kim Jong-il; the colour purple stands for Kim Il-sung (there is a purple orchid called Kimilsungia) and red for Kim Jong-il (a red begonia carries the name Kimjongilia). When a snowy mountain and a lake are shown, they refer to Paektu Mountain, the invented birthplace of Kim Jong-il. The new North Korean religion took over old elements from its ancient mythology just as Christianity appropriated pagan beliefs: Paektu Mountain was also the birthplace of the Korean race.

Interpreted in this way, it all starts to make sense. The tie between North Koreans and their Leaders is not just political, but also religious. One does wonder how this will evolve in the future. Facts don't lie: the 'gods' did not protect their flock from great suffering. Kim Il-sung sensibly died just before the famine struck, so in the public's memory he is untainted by it. Kim Jong-il was less fortunate, but his portrait was nonetheless added to his father's when he died. How will Kim III fare?

Next we are shepherded onto a real tram. The carriages are clean and spacious and festooned with little flags and plastic flowers in our honour. North Koreans are of course not allowed to join us on the tram. We pass dirty buses with passengers crammed together like sardines in a tin.

It is again striking how well the apartment buildings look from afar. The architecture is pared down, simple, stark and grand. The paint almost makes them pretty. At some point I see a hill, right in the middle of town, that has three villas on it. I wonder who lives there. I don't think they are 'workers'. As the pigs who control the government in Orwell's *Animal Farm* say: 'All animals are equal, but some animals are more equal than others.'

The quasi-religious iconography comes to the fore again, and along the way we notice countless public buildings with large portraits of the two leaders above their front entrances. By law, the size of the portraits needs to be commensurate with the size of the building.

The making of a totalitarian dynasty came about through a mix of historical circumstances, cunning, violence and regular purges to keep potential competitors for power on the straight and narrow. Purging continues right up to this day: five out of the seven civilian and military pallbearers at Kim Jong-il's funeral in December 2011 were purged within two years. The new Great Leader was simply taking a leaf out of his grandfather's book. History is continuously rewritten, just as it was in Orwell's Ministry of Truth, wherein the dictatorship had the names of those who were purged retroactively deleted from official records.

Kim Il-sung was born in 1912 in Japanese-occupied Korea. In 1920 he moved with his family to Manchuria. In 1935 Kim allegedly joined the Northeast Anti-Japanese United Army, a guerrilla group led by the Chinese Communist Party. He was a commissar responsible for political ideology in a guerrilla group of about 160 soldiers: a mid-ranking function. He was not involved in actual fighting. In 1937, when he was twenty-four, he was allegedly appointed commander of the 88th Brigade and was thus responsible for a few hundred men. By 1940 the Japanese had decimated the guerrillas so successfully that Kim was their last surviving leader. He fled to the Soviet Union, where he was trained and he became a major in the Red Army until the end of the Second World War.

When Japan vacated Korea, the Soviet Union searched for a pliable Korean to head the North Korean puppet state. There were virtually no communists extant in North Korea. Kim Il-sung was only their fourth choice.* It was the notorious Lavrentiy Beria, Soviet chief of police (including the gulag), who in the end recommended 33-year-old Kim Il-sung to Stalin. Kim had the required characteristics: Korean-born, Russian-speaking, educated in Russia and a communist of long-standing. Kim was inexperienced:

---

* The first choice was Cho Man-sik, who was the most admired political figure in Korea. A Christian nationalist, he had actively resisted the Japanese and had for example refused to adopt a Japanese name in the 1940s. Now he refused to collaborate with the Soviets. The next choice was Pak Hon-yong, leader of the Korean Communist Party. Unfortunately he was from the capital Seoul in South Korea and had little support in the North; Stalin refused to appoint him (he was later executed on the orders of Kim Il-sung). Third choice was Kim Mu-chong, who had participated in the Long March with Mao, and was an eloquent speaker and great leader. The Soviets distrusted him because he was too close to China.

the most he had done with his 88th Brigade was to cross the border on 4 June 1937, kill a few Japanese police officers and extract food for the road back. It's a far cry from the invented North Korean history which asserts that Kim Il-sung more or less single-handedly repelled the Japanese from Korea.

One month after the Japanese withdrawal, the Soviets brought Kim to the port city of Wonsan. He was introduced to the people at a mass rally in Pyongyang, but it was a disaster: the people had expected to meet a redoubtable warrior, and instead saw a youth with a haircut like a Chinese waiter who made an uninspiring speech in creaky Korean. The Soviets stuck to their choice. Kim Il-sung became Premier in 1948 and Chairman of the Workers' Party of Korea in 1949.

From 1945 to 1950, North Korea was under the direct and complete control of Moscow. Kim needed explicit approval for all he did. The Soviets wrote the North Korean Constitution, and Stalin even amended it by hand. Three Soviet generals decided what the exact composition of the North Korean Parliament would be, while the Soviet Politburo set the Parliament's agenda. The Soviets redistributed the land among the peasants through the Land Reform Act. The main industries were nationalised. There were several rebellions against the Soviet occupation, and the Soviets arrested the opposition. As there was no North Korean gulag yet, those arrested were either killed or sent to camps in Siberia. About 15 per cent of the North Korean population fled to South Korea.

Kim's invasion of South Korea in 1950 was a disaster and, after suffering tremendous losses, an Armistice was signed under which the border more or less reverted to where it had been before. North

Korea's invented history describes the war as a resounding victory and Kim the undisputed hero. His son Kim Jong-il later recalled the memoirs of other revolutionary leaders to make sure no contradictory accounts were left in circulation.

After the war, Kim promoted those who had joined the Workers' Party during the war, as well as former friends from the guerrillas. As new leaders the world over know, the advantage of favouring 'new men' is that they owe allegiance only to the new leader. Everyone who threatened Kim's exercise of totalitarian power was purged. Soviet influence waned as the USSR had not actively fought in the war. Pro-Soviet party leaders were purged. Those who had formed the communist resistance during the Japanese occupation were accused of being Japanese spies, and shot or sent to concentration camps. It didn't stop there: of the ten people who had constituted the North Korean Politburo in 1949, three were purged and shot; two were purged and disappeared; two were killed in the Korean War, and one was exiled and briefly returned in the 1980s. Only Kim Il-sung and one other former Politburo member died of natural causes.

Mao's China, with its utopian beliefs in self-sacrifice by the workers and total submission to its Great Helmsman, was seen as a far more desirable model to emulate than the wimps in Khrushchev's 'liberal' Kremlin. Kim loved Mao's vision of a regimented economy where all is owned by the state, and in the gift of the munificent Leader. Food, jobs, healthcare and housing would be distributed to all by the state. Workers were urged to break production levels selflessly. Capitalist profiteering would end. The Leader's word became law, sometimes literally: when Kim Jong-il once casually observed that 'women should wear national dress', for a while this was actually enforced.

North Korea would become self-sufficient, and foreign meddling in its affairs would end. Soviet advisors were sent packing. Foreigners who had married North Koreans were expelled, and their spouses were forced to divorce them.

One foreign import North Korea did not reject was aid – at least, the regime never admitted receiving it. First, Kim engaged China and the Soviet Union in a bidding war for his favour. Both needed North Korea as a buffer against South Korea and the United States, and both sent massive amounts of aid. When the Soviet Union and the Eastern Block opted for capitalism in the 1990s, their support ended, but China made up for the shortfall. Perhaps the Chinese leaders were grateful for the support North Korea's dictator had given to its leaders during the Tiananmen Square Massacre.

Outwardly, a semblance of democracy is upheld. The Constitution guarantees universal and direct suffrage by secret ballot for the Supreme People's Assembly and the lower assemblies. In reality, people are told how to vote by their *inminban*; and woe betide he who does not turn up to vote. On polling day the stations are supervised by the State Security Department. One can vote only for or against the one proposed candidate: if one is 'for', one does not need to do anything; one can just drop the paper in the ballot box. To vote 'against' the candidate, one needs to draw a circle around the candidate's name. No pencils are provided and nobody in his right mind even thinks of going into the partitioned-off polling booth. All the proposed candidates are elected with a 100 per cent turnout.

Kim Il-sung adopted an increasingly tyrannical lifestyle: his food came exclusively from private farms; officials made him gifts of women and palaces; and his son Kim Jong-il took to kneeling to take his father's shoes off. When he defected, Kim Il-sung's doctor, Kim So-yeon, claimed that the Great Leader enjoyed regular blood transfusions from men and women in their twenties in a bid to live to 100. Transfusions of young blood to conquer old age, as described in Aldous Huxley's dystopian *Brave New World*, had apparently become fact.

After the tram ride the group is split up between those who have paid $100 extra to do a helicopter flight above Pyongyang, and us mere mortals who will go on one more city trip. The drawback of the latter choice is that the *Gruppenführerin* will be on our coach.

We drive through a large concrete gate (the Great Leaders are watching us from above) into the Mansudae Art Studios, a light industrial complex that houses a number of artists' collectives. These were set up in 1959 to produce art glorifying Kim Il-sung. First we visit the painters. The entrance hall features a large oil portrait of Kim Il-sung. After that, it's three floors of gaudy canvases with bucolic landscapes, struggling workers, and portraits of the Leaders. There is definitely a state-sanctioned style. The minder on the first floor says we can photograph the works; the minder of the second floor says we cannot photograph the works; and the minder on the third floor allows it again.

Mrs Kim tries to rationalise this: 'The paintings on the second floor are made by very famous artists.' It's all the same saccharine, formulaic mediocrity to me.

Next it's the turn of the pottery studios. The entrance hall features a large photo portrait of Kim Il-sung. Previous visitors have left a few bouquets of now-wilting flowers beneath the portrait. I wonder whether they bowed, too. In every studio in the building, the same mud-coloured vases are produced. The artists are at work and don't even glance at us; they must have been told not to do so. Apart from some scratching and use of materials and us scuffling around, there is silence.

A short drive brings us to the Embroidery House. This is a pretty building with a pagoda roof. The Embroidery House has a large, embroidered portrait of Kim Il-sung in its entrance. Then it's up the stairs to visit two rooms where women are ruining their eyes embroidering elaborate works featuring tigers and the like. Piles of gaudy balls of wool are on tables in front of them. The women are all elaborately wrapped up: the heating isn't working, and it's cold. Somebody with more money than taste will perhaps buy their works.

When we come out of the Embroidery House we take a good look at the famous 105-storey Ryugyong Hotel, which looms over it like a malevolent pyramid.

Had it been opened in 1989 as planned, it would have been the highest hotel in the world. Allegedly, it was Kim Jong-il's mother who fired him on to build high. There is a quasi-biblical story doing the rounds in invented Korean history. One day in 1948, Kim I and his mother stood on a hill overlooking Pyongyang. Mama Kim expressed admiration for the tall buildings rising where previously low houses had stood. She said that he 'should build many tall buildings, of thirty or forty floors high'.

'I will build buildings of 100 floors,' he replied.

Thirty-nine years after its commencement, the Ryugyong remains unfinished and stands empty. It symbolises all that is wrong with North Korea. The construction cost 2 per cent of North Korea's GDP. Building it was always a strange priority, as even in the 'model city' of Pyongyang hospitals still don't have incubators. There was an attempt to attract foreign capital, with promises of 'inside anything goes', but too few foreigners took the bait. Serious trouble started when the Soviet Union abandoned communism and aid to North Korea. The behemoth stood empty for decades without windows, and with a rusting crane on top at 300m high. The official censors made sure it never featured in any official photos. In the late 1990s an inspection from the European Union concluded that the building was irreparable: the concrete was sub-quality and the lift shafts weren't straight.

The unsightliness may well have been the main reason to put in the windows in 2011. They were paid for by the Egyptian telecoms company Orascom.*

The Ryugyong was to open partially in 2012 on the 100th anniversary of Kim Il-sung's birth, but that was cancelled. In 2013 the

---

* But why did an Egyptian telecoms company pay for the windows? Orascom set up a joint venture called Koryolink, in which the state-owned Korea Post and Telecommunications Corporation has a 25 per cent share, to develop the sole 3G network in North Korea. There are now more than 2.5 million mobile phones. The phones are said to be North Korean-made, but are in fact rebranded Chinese ones, officially running on 'Juche Software'. A mobile phone must be paid in foreign currency and usually costs a hefty $200. The elites' phones start with a specific number and they pay less for their calls. The phones are used by many new businessmen: it allows them to communicate prices for goods in other parts of the country quickly, and this has led to market prices evening out and supply meeting demand more easily. The mobile phones are also seen as a status symbol. Koryolink texts are monitored in real time, so the venture must have given a tremendous boost to North Korean employment.

international hotel chain Kempinski again cancelled the opening because of yet another military crisis between North Korea and the rest of the world. Recently it has been claimed that the workers are supplied with methamphetamines to work harder.

The approach of the lunchtime restaurant requires additional admonitions from the other group's *Gruppenführerin*: 'Our lunch will be in a restaurant in a residential complex. Do not approach the people who live there because they are not used to foreigners. Do not photograph them: they won't like it. You have to stay inside the restaurant!'

It's located in a narrow street; a bit of an exception in a city where even alleyways seem to be 10m wide. It's the closest we've been allowed to walk to residential housing. The handful of locals on their way to the building site, where they work twelve-hour shifts for no pay, stop in their tracks to have a good look at us. No stones are thrown, nobody spits and a friendly wave is promptly returned with a wave and a broad smile.

Upstairs, we take seats at one long table. A number of little gold bowls with tiny amounts of different food already wait for us. Mrs Kim explains that the number of food bowls indicates the importance of the guest. Eleven bowls represent a meal for a king. An eleventh bowl is duly added. This traditional set-up is called *pan-sanggi*; but for some translucent noodles seasoned with pepper, I care for none of it. Cold buckwheat noodles are a North Korean delicacy. It's also a typical wedding dish; when a North Korean asks his friend when he will marry, the literal translation of the question is: 'When can I eat your cold noodles?' Pyongyang's most famous cold noodle restaurant, Okryugwan, which seats 2,000, operates with ration coupons that one can try to obtain via one's work unit for a hefty bribe.

We also get the usual fluoro-pink kimchi as well as pickles, seaweed, a pan-fried boiled egg from a starved chicken, vegetables and many non-identifiable foodstuffs. Later, when the rest is eaten, a bowl of rice arrives. For some reason bland cooked rice always arrives *after* a meal is consumed. It's as if they are saying: 'And if you gluttonous Westerners are still hungry after this feast, then stuff yourselves with some dry rice.'

The meal drags on. The helicopter flight undertaken by the other group is taking far longer than expected and we therefore have to be kept entertained. And lo, Christmas lights are switched on, and two waitresses in short skirts start singing love songs from a stage covered in tin-foil. Occasionally the amplifier emits deafening shrieks, perhaps to keep us awake. North Koreans much prefer silly love songs such as 'Nice to Meet You' to all the other tunes that extol the greatness of the Kims. Soon the singing waitresses pick my fellow travellers to join them on the stage. When my mates start to call out my name I claim an urgent need for the loo and disappear, leaving their laughter behind. After I've spent an eternity in the cubicle, I hurry down the stairs and out of the building. I quite fancy a little illegal walk around the block, but Mr Chong suddenly pops up out of nowhere and orders me not to venture beyond the edge of the pavement 2m away. I go back inside and waste some time visiting the small supermarket at the bottom of the stairs. It sells lots of bizarre food, including what looks like dried octopus. There is other meat of dubious faunal provenance.

Upstairs the karaoke has finished. The entire restaurant did the conga in the end. One must admit that it's a bit odd to dance after lunch in the daylight.

CHAPTER FIVE

FIRING MISSILES WHILE
THE PEOPLE STARVE

Unsurprisingly, the Stamp Museum's entrance hall features a large portrait of Kim Il-sung. On the first floor is an exhibition of the thousands of stamps that North Korea has issued over the years. With stamp-collecting falling out of fashion, the national missile budget must have been severely depleted. Every possible subject that any possible collector in any possible country in the world could desire has been printed: Charles and Diana's wedding day; a series of cats looking at frogs; a stamp celebrating the election victory of French socialist President Mitterrand in 1981; Kaiser Wilhelm II for the more military-inclined collector; and stamps featuring different kinds of food. The latter are probably not aimed at the home market. When I ask for a stamp with Margaret Thatcher, I draw a blank. Behind the counter I spot a small, kitschy pewter Kim Il-sung statue. It would make for an excellent joke present, but at $200, I pass.

The shop is most interesting for its postcards. Drab council estates and the monument of the Korean Workers' Party are hot subjects. There are also colourful posters featuring boots crushing

America, nuclear missiles, hip Molotov-cocktail-throwing youths, and Korean slogans in red with exclamation marks. My travel companions buy these by the dozen. The running joke is that we will send these postcards to our enemies in the West who will then get into trouble with their Security Services (three weeks later I duly receive one at home in London signed 'X').

Not enough time has yet been used up of our short trip. If you run out of tyranny heritage sites, what is there left to visit? Mrs Kim takes us across the street to the Koryo Hotel, which, with 500 rooms, is the second largest in Pyongyang. It was built in 1985 and is strictly off-limits for North Koreans unless they work there, are on official business or bribe the doorman. In fact, it abuts a high-rise neighbourhood of Pyongyang where the Central Committee Members reside, and is a no-go area for ordinary Pyongyangites. When, a few years ago, even in this elite district hot water provision was rationed to two times, two hours a day, many communist cadres moved into the Koryo Hotel permanently.

The hotel consists of two towers linked at the top by a corridor. This symbolises the reunification of Korea under the Kims. By international standards it's three stars at most, but North Korea proudly declares it holds five. Amenities include a pool, a sauna, two cinemas, a hairdresser, a casino, a ping-pong room, a billiard room, a gym, tailor, shoe-maker, beauty salon, karaoke, screen golf and several shops. There is no internet access. The hotel was constructed with the benefit of on-the-spot guidance from Kim Il-sung to showcase 'the greatness of the DPRK'. When a fire broke out in 2015, the tourists who tried to take photos were arrested.

The marble reception hall is cavernous and sombre. In the back is a curious non-functioning fountain featuring coloured lights. On the first floor is an equally dimly lit bookshop that sells the works of the Kims and mud-coloured pottery. The prices in the shop are more expensive than in central London. I buy a medal for the marathon I didn't run for $40.

An hour later we are on our way to the Demilitarized Zone (DMZ) and the city of Kaesong. The motorway is truly massive: a wide concrete expanse piercing the landscape in a straight line towards the border, but not past it. It is empty of traffic, no doubt because North Koreans need a special permit to use it.

Not only where you live, but also where you travel is strictly controlled in North Korea. The regime wants to prevent people from obtaining information from elsewhere, so a North Korean needs a permit from the police to travel to a city or county that does not have a common border with the city or county where he is registered; or for overnight travel. The permit states the reason of travel and the traveller has to produce the permit when he stays overnight at a hotel or with friends. If caught travelling without it, he can be arrested and punished with a fine or a penalty of forced labour. Obtaining a normal permit typically takes two to three days, but a special permit to travel to restricted areas, such as Pyongyang or any area near the South Korean or Chinese border, takes seven to fifteen days and needs to be approved by the Ministry of State Security. Interestingly, those who live in Pyongyang, and who therefore largely belong to the Reliable Class, have a special Pyongyang citizen ID card that grants them greater rights to travel away from the capital. Travel permits are checked (together with one's identity card) on motorways or in trains every time a provincial border is crossed.

At the height of the famine, travel permits for Pyongyang were tightened up: the dictatorship did not want the population to see that food provision was prioritised for Pyongyang residents. At the same time, the travel-permit system collapsed as officials needed money too, and became susceptible to bribes. Indeed today, a licence to go to Pyongyang costs about thirty dollars in bribes. Travel is now most often done for private trade: to buy and sell goods elsewhere.

But even with a travel permit, criss-crossing the country is not a regular pursuit, since the ramshackle nature of public transport and the roads make it very time-consuming. The few individuals who make trips in cars or lorries rent out their spare seats privately.

In the absence of any noticeable demand for motorways, why was this one built?

The penny drops when we come across tank traps: large concrete cubes left and right of the motorway that can be blown up to block it for oncoming traffic. The road's name is also a bit of a giveaway: it's called the Reunification Highway. In North Korea, reunification only ever means one thing: that the Kims' rule is expanded over the entire peninsula. This motorway would be very handy to send tanks to the border and across it; or if you needed extra landing strips for, say, military jets. It was finished in 1992 and is now full of potholes. The lane markings have long disappeared.

Here and there the coach has to avoid small groups of workers crouching around cauldrons. They are filling up the potholes one at a time. Some people are picnicking on the kerbside. A surprising number of folks are just hanging about. Have they all decided to pull a sickie?

We are waved through the multiple control points where travel permits are checked. Mrs Kim always warns us well in advance when we approach one, as it's advisable to hide our cameras from the soldiers. We are again and again told not to photograph any soldiers or military installations.

Red earth and dramatic hills dazzle in the afternoon light. We come across long-established villages with traditional whitewashed houses with grey pagoda-style tiled roofs. The land is laboured by way of ploughs and oxen. Every square metre of land is utilised, but we can't see whether what they grow will reach the bountiful harvests Western-engineered seeds provide. There aren't any trees; only hills so steep that they would be unusable for agriculture actually have some dark green tree cover.

'The farmers don't want trees eating the nutrients that could help grow potatoes,' Mrs Kim knows.

In fact, during the economic crisis of the 1990s, all trees were chopped up for firewood – or for human consumption. When the Soviet Union became capitalist and China started to reform its economy, they stopped delivering cheap fuel to North Korea. China, for example, used to provide three-quarters of North Korea's fuel. So, in a country with regular frosts of minus thirty, the trees had to go.* The trunks of some surviving trees are painted

---

* In winter it is also impossible to get post in North Korea as post workers burn the letters for warmth.

white to indicate that they are government property, and off-bounds for firewood.

Incidentally, I didn't spot a single animal in North Korea. The dog-eating tradition is of course well known (the Korean word for spicy dog-meat stew is *boshintang*). But during the famine, *all* animals were eaten, including songbirds. The frog population has more or less been wiped out, too. In the monsoon, entire villages wait along rivers with lights to catch the mountain frogs when they come down. The frogs are eaten, dried to eat later, or sold to Chinese customers. The oil in the frog's stomach is siphoned off to make choice frog oil.

Hungry locals used to find some food by digging up shellfish from beaches, fishing and gathering seaweed. One day, the government fenced off the beaches: officially to keep out spies; in reality to increase the take by the state fishing fleet. The fish they catch is sold abroad to pay for the missiles programme and the Kims' luxuries. Recently Kim III introduced rewards to increase sea fishing. Since then, a large number of ghost ships with dead bodies on board have been found off the Japanese coast. The lure of the state rewards is so great that North Koreans go fishing on whatever vessel they can lay their hands on, regardless of its seaworthiness. They do not have GPS, and often get lost in the rough seas.

We halt for a comfort break at a building that bridges the motorway. It has a certain 1950s *je ne sais quoi*. The concrete structure is apparently a tourist destination, as we can't find any petrol or locals here. For some reason the restaurant and shop inside the building are not used – perhaps there is no electricity? Outside in the empty parking lot, trestle-tables covered with peony table-cloths exhibit a few meagre goodies for sale. For ten dollars I buy a bottle of alcohol with a small snake inside.

'It's made of Soju, Korean rice-liquor. You can find snake wine in China and Vietnam as well,' Australian Pete knows. 'The live snake is pushed in the bottle with alcohol and then drowns when the stop is put in. In a last attempt to escape, the snake wiggles its head into the neck of the bottle.'

Mine does indeed have its head up.

'The punters prefer it when the snakes are venomous, to have the venom dissolve in the liquor. It's a macho thing. In reality the liquor renders the poison inactive. The recipe is from 1000 BC; the Chinese invented it.'

I also buy an apple. Fruit is not easily obtained, except in the main hotel in Pyongyang. The saleswoman is perhaps 4ft 5in and she is not suffering from dwarfism. She looks like she is about thirty years old, so she must have grown up during the worst of the famine. Malnutrition was so bad for so long that the army had to reduce its minimum height restriction for new recruits. Today, the average seventeen-year-old South Korean male is five inches taller than a North Korean defector of the same age. All over North Korea, you see young adults who are the size of children.

Back on the motorway we suddenly see about 1,000 bicycles parked in a field. Up the hill, the owners of the bicycles are crouched together in a group. Six very large speakers strapped to a lorry harangue them. Are we witnessing one of the thrice-weekly indoctrination lessons every North Korean has to attend? In the next days, time and again we come across groups of between twenty and several hundred people gathered in public spaces for no apparent reason. I mean, there is no concert or festival going on. They just crouch there, and have the regime's political inanities shouted at them.

Not only are North Koreans obliged to work and are allocated a job by the state, they also have no control over their spare time. To begin with, informal socialising between four or more people, e.g. a chess club or a book club, is illegal. Every North Korean is required to participate in organisations in their leisure time. This makes it easier for the state to keep an eye on them, and to make sure that they keep an eye on each other. It starts with the compulsory attendance of a kindergarten. From the age of fourteen onwards almost every North Korean is a member of the Kim Il-sung Youth League. From the age of eighteen, they can apply to become a member of the Workers' Party of Korea.* Later in life, one has to join the Agricultural Union, the Trade Union or, for housewives, the Women's Union.

These bodies 'educate' their members three times a week, with each session lasting up to two hours. The sessions take place in special 'Revolutionary Rooms'. Two of the sessions are ideological, and the attendees are told about the great deeds or utterances of the Leader; about the awfulness of the American imperialists and how the South Koreans suffer under the American imperialists' jackboot; about the Workers' Party of Korea; about the Juche

---

* One's party member application is proposed by two party members of good standing. This is then discussed at a plenary session of a Party Cell and ratified by a county-level party committee.

ideology; or about the great industrial and technological advances of North Korea. As homework they may have to learn the Supreme Leaders' speeches by heart. The speeches cover a wide variety of practical subjects from 'how to prepare for war' and 'how to keep an eye on foreigners in the country'; right up to 'the advantages of brushing one's teeth regularly', or detailed instructions on 'how rice seedlings should be protected with plastic sheeting'. It is all rather similar to the 'Two Minutes Hate' in *Nineteen Eighty-Four*. It figures: Orwell found his inspirations in the constant rallies haranguing Soviet Russians during the Stalin era; and North Korea is, if anything, profoundly Stalinist. One session a week is dedicated to self-criticism, wherein a person is singled out publicly to confess his wrongs and another attendee then openly criticises him for whatever misdeeds he can come up with – and so the people keep each other in check. People try to cope with these sessions by keeping their heads down so as not to be the next target. They are well-versed in admitting the most anodyne of 'sins'.

The compulsory-membership organisations mobilise their members for the mass rallies. On 5 May 2016, for example, the organisations made sure that all citizens were gathered the next day at 9 a.m. to watch a special live broadcast of the 7th Korean Workers' Party Congress. Just a pity that the precise timing of the broadcast was not announced: people simply had to wait till it came on many hours later.

Does it come as a surprise that the main North Korean hobby is drinking? Since the famine, things have loosened up somewhat. It is now possible to avoid attendance by paying a bribe or by paying professionals to attend these meetings in one's place. There is even a word for these people: they are called 'rear-area units'.

Soon after, we arrive in Kaesong. Kaesong was the capital of the Korean Kingdom of Taebong from the tenth century onwards; and later of the Koryo Kingdom. Today it is a medium-sized city of 200,000 people. It is grey and features only a few tall buildings. Kaesong is the only city that was handed from South to North Korea under the 1953 Armistice (the new border varied very little from the old one).* What strikes us is the militant ambience: there are red flags everywhere, and oversized boards with slogans in the Korean circle-and-stripes alphabet.** Loudspeakers boom at the locals. This border town still enthusiastically perceives itself as being at war sixty-three years after hostilities with the South ended. It is not unlike the Perpetual State of War, which in *Nineteen Eighty-Four* served to distract from home-grown problems. About half the population is in uniform. No one is smiling. With 1.2 million soldiers, almost 6 million paramilitary and 600,000 reserves, North Korea has the highest per-capita army in the world. Kaesong used to be famous for its ginseng production, but now it focuses on industry. Or it *did*. In February, 54,000 North Koreans lost their jobs after Kim III announced that he had tested a hydrogen bomb. How did this come about?

It all started with the election of Kim Dae-jung as president of South Korea in 1998. He was in favour of a détente with North

---

* The new border was drawn south of the Thirty-Eighth Parallel to the west; and north of the parallel to the east of the Korean peninsula towards the Sea of Japan.

** The Korean alphabet is unique and not shared by any other language.

Korea. His biography reads like an implausible political soap:* he ended up owning the company where he started working as a clerk before he was elected to the National Assembly. He was later persecuted by the South Korean dictatorship but eventually elected to the presidency.

Kim Dae-jung's main brainchild was the Sunshine Policy, which attempted to thaw relations with North Korea. The policy's name came from *The North Wind and the Sun*, one of Aesop's Fables, in which the north wind and the sun compete with each other to see who is the strongest. The north wind (hard-line policy) is unable to blow the coat off a traveller, but the heat of the sunshine (a policy of détente) made the traveller take off his coat.

Kim Dae-jung's desire for better relations with the North came as a godsend to Kim Jong-il: by 1999 the famine was in its fifth year, and he urgently needed foreign aid to keep his grip on power.

North Korea agreed to organise some reunions between North and South Korean families who had been cut off from each other since the Korean War. North Korea received fertiliser and food aid in return.

---

* Kim Dae-jung was born in a middle-class farming family. He started working as a clerk in a formerly Japanese-owned shipping company, and ended up owning it. A talented orator, he was first elected representative for the National Assembly in 1961, but the elections were voided by General Park Chung-Hee's military coup. Kim again won seats in the Assembly in 1963 and 1967. He stood for the presidency in 1971, but lost to Park. He was almost killed during a kidnap attempt in Tokyo by Park's security services in 1973. Kim was banned from politics; imprisoned for signing an anti-dictatorship manifesto; and later put under house arrest. When Park was assassinated in 1979, Kim got his political rights back, but was sentenced to death on charges of sedition. Both Pope John Paul II and the US government intervened, and he was sent into exile to the USA where he lectured at Harvard University. When he returned to South Korea in 1985, he was again put under house arrest. Kim Dae-jung stood for the presidency in the first democratic elections in 1987, but the opposition vote was split between two candidates, and the government candidate Roh Tae-woo won. After the economy collapsed in the wake of the Asian Economic Crisis in 1998 the public vented its anger by finally electing Kim Dae-jung president.

Next Kim Dae-jung asked for a summit with the North. Kim Jong-il demanded a $500 million up-front payment in return. It was duly wired. This led to the historic meeting of the two leaders in 2000, which in turn led to joint business ventures. Kim received the Nobel Peace Prize for his Sunshine Policy in 2000. It apparently costs $500 million.

The Kaesong Industrial Zone was one of the joint ventures resulting from the summit. A South Korean business group leased the land near Kaesong for a term of fifty years. Small and medium South Korean companies were enticed to set up factories by way of cheap loans and guarantees from the South Korean government. Because of these, they risked little from North Korea's erratic behaviour. North Korea provided the cheap labour.

The Zone opened its doors in 2002. Initially the Zone produced clothes, shoes and watches. By 2016, some 54,000 North Koreans were employed there. Wild predictions of potentially 700,000 workers or more were routinely floated. Around 800 South Koreans lived in the Zone, and many more commuted daily from South Korea via direct rail and road routes.

The North Korean workers' wages, amounting to $90 million, were paid directly to the North Korean government. Cynics said that North Korea farmed out its population and netted the proceeds. But even though the North Korean dictatorship handed only about 30 per cent back to them, it still meant that they earned significantly more than their compatriots. Everybody gained from the arrangement.

However much the North Korean profited from the Zone, the

Kims were not about to give up on their nuclear ambitions. They were firmly determined to have their cake and eat it. They miscalculated: the Kims' missile tests caused the Kaesong Industrial Zone to be closed three times in 2009. The recent 2013 incident was more serious. Just to give a flavour of the tension in the peninsula, here follows a concise timeline since 2012:

- In December 2012 Kim III tests a missile. The United Nations issue sanctions.
- In February 2013 Kim III announces a new nuclear and long-range missile test, and declares martial law. On 12 February an artificial earth tremor confirms that North Korea tested a nuclear weapon. North Korea tells China that it will test two more nuclear weapons that year in order to bring the USA to the negotiating table. In passing, North Korea also threatens the final destructions of South Korea by way of a pre-emptive strike.
- In March North Korea aims its long-range missiles at the USA in retaliation for recent UN sanctions. The USA increases its intercepting missiles.
- On 20 March North Korea organises a cyber-attack against South Korea. Japan deploys destroyers carrying its ballistic missile defence system in the East China Sea.
- On 27 March North Korea interrupts the direct communications hotline with the South saying that 'war can break out at any moment'. The USA flies stealth bombers with nuclear capacity over North Korea. North Korea declares a state of war against South Korea (which is presumably more serious than

the 'permanent state of war readiness' that North Korea says has existed since the Korean War).

- Western media say that North Korea's rhetoric is not to be taken seriously as long as the Kaesong Industrial Zone is open. On 3 April NK removes its 54,000 workers from the Zone and closes the complex. North Korea says that it has ratified a merciless attack against the United States. It advises foreign embassies to leave North Korea by 10 April.

- North Korea suddenly accepts China's offer to mediate. South Korea rejects talks, allowing the North to claim that South Korean warmongers don't want peace.

- On 1 May North Korea condemns the American Kenneth Bae to fifteen years of hard labour for proselytising, planning a coup d'état and setting up bases in China to topple the North Korean dictatorship. Apparently Bae had photographed starving children.

- On 18 and 19 May North Korea launches four short-range missiles into the Sea of Japan.

- On 6 June North Korea proposes official talks with South Korea regarding the Kaesong Industrial Zone. South Korea accepts. The hotline is restored; the six-party talks are restarted; and on 16 September Kaesong is reopened.

- On 8 October North Korea puts its army on alert. South Korea is threatened with merciless attacks if it doesn't stop the air drops of anti-Pyongyang leaflets.

- In January 2016 a tremor is felt in China and South Korea. North Korea declares that it just successfully detonated a hydrogen bomb. International experts say that it was merely a boosted atomic bomb.

- On 10 February 2016 South Korea announces the withdrawal from the Kaesong Industrial Zone after North Korea carries out a ballistic missile test. South Korea says it does not want the financial profits of Kaesong to be used for the North's development of nuclear weapons. A day later the South Koreans leave Kaesong within hours of North Korea expelling them. South Korea follows this up by shutting off electricity and water to Kaesong.

- The 54,000 North Korean workers at Kaesong have been unemployed since then. I guess they could be redeployed in Kim's reforestation campaign.

Over the decades, North Korea has ratcheted up tensions on the Korean peninsula again and again. Every time, the situation normalises again, until the next incident. It happens so regularly that the West no longer takes it seriously. Let's face it: North Korea's missiles tend to be inaccurate; the South Korean population is twice that of North Korea; and North Korea has no friends left who would offer military support for an invasion of the South. Were it to invade the South, North Korea would be crushed like a fly. Why then does it keep creating tension?

In fact, its reasons are perfectly rational: as I mentioned before, the permanent state of war allows the regime to stay in power. North Koreans are naturally suspicious of Americans since the Korean War. By and large, they are willing to follow the Great

Leader of the day against their enemy, and to suffer some of the loss of freedom and material wealth and the garrison economy that does with it. By regularly ratcheting up tension, and by repeating every day that they are at war with the American imperialists, the Japanese war criminals and the puppet regime in the South, the regime keeps it grip on the country. For decades, foreign liberal commentators have announced that North Korea is opening up, and that change is imminent. In reality, the regime is still firmly in command, using the old Stalinist methods that have been discarded everywhere else in the world.

But how has North Korea managed to survive economically?

The answer is largely by way of foreign aid – and this has been achieved through its foreign policy as well. For the first forty-five years of its existence the country received huge volumes of aid from fellow communist countries, as it was at the edge of the communist-capitalist geographical dividing line. China and the Soviet Union were played off against each other, and North Korea maximised the aid it received from them.

But how to extract military and food aid after the Soviet Union and China stopped being hard-line communist countries in the 1990s? This was achieved by the regular escalation of military tension. On the one hand, military tension reminds China that if the North Korean regime falls, it would effectively share a border with the USA. So China continues to support the regime, be it reluctantly and in moderation. On the other hand, the military tension alarms the USA, Japan and South Korea; and they are willing to pay a price to avoid it. Take North Korea's nuclear ambitions, for example. Now that China and Russia would probably not automatically support it, nobody believes that North Korea could win a conventional war against the South and the USA. So North Korea develops nuclear devices. Their effectiveness, and the effectiveness of the ballistic missiles that are supposed to carry them, is questionable. But the USA, Japan and South Korea cannot run the risk. So at several times in the past twenty years they have bought North Korea off with aid. This tactic has worked again and again.

The pattern is always the same: the North ratchets up the hostile rhetoric; threatens to nuke the USA, Japan and South Korea; ends all cooperation; announces a state of war etc. The West responds by increasing military activity, and through sanctions. And every single time the West ends up making concessions to North Korea to reduce the tension by way of aid or trade. The situation then normalises until North Korea sets off on another bout of nuclear blackmail.

We have arrived at the hotel in Kaesong.

'Please do not leave the hotel!' Mr Chong warns.

So we take some photos in the twilight while the gates of the compound are still open and we can still discern some of the even less free world beyond. Both the neighbourhood and the Minsok Folk Hotel are built in traditional Korean style, and we are told that at least part of the hotel is more than 100 years old. Around the courtyard are some low buildings used as an office and a shop. The shop sells the works of the Kims in four languages, and mud-coloured pottery. In the midst of the complex is a narrow stream with a number of low traditional houses on either side, and bridges connecting the two. Each house has a little courtyard with four en-suite bedrooms. The house is single storey: it has white walls with brown beams and a grey pagoda-style roof. We are to take our shoes off and leave them outside, Japanese-style. The two doors are covered in rice paper and opened with a padlock with one key for the two of us. The main room is a living room during the day, and in the evening flat mattresses are unrolled into beds. There is an *ondol*, the under-floor heating system that the Koreans claim to have invented (never mind the Romans). This uses hot water from thermoelectric power plants. When the power plants don't work, which is often, *ondols* can freeze and burst. A single lightbulb dangles from the ceiling. The television doesn't work and the bathroom features a rusting bath-tub that won't produce warm water in the morning.

Outside the dining room we have to take our shoes off, too. We sit down on cushions on the floor, and the food is served on a low table. Two women in national hoop-dress discreetly shuffle around to serve us. The only things missing are a Japanese hairdo, geisha make-up and a Japanese koto player in the corner. Ironically, Korea has always been heavily influenced by Japan.

When North Korea wasn't doing too badly in the 1960s, it attracted 100,000 Koreans who had up to then had been living in Japan. Their much fanfared return to the homeland was called 'the Great Movement of the Korean People' and was used by communist media worldwide to prove that people chose socialism over capitalism. Their money and higher standards of living provoked admiration and jealousy. They brought electrical goods and furniture with them that North Koreans were not even aware existed. They even had enough money to buy cars. For a short while all things Japanese became fashionable, which was surprising as by then the North Koreans had been subjected to fifteen years of propaganda portraying the Japanese as evil colonisers, and North Korean products as the best in the world. There followed a jealous backlash: the immigrants from Japan were ranked as 'complex' in the class system, making it impossible for them to obtain good jobs. They were forbidden from driving white cars, as from the air 'they would look like the white in a Japanese flag'. Unless they still had family in Japan who regularly sent them money and goods, many slowly started to sell off possession and became as poor as everybody else.

We have been asked in advance whether we want to try 'sweet meat' i.e. dog. Half the group howl in disgust and look sick; the others have a bowl with soup put in front of them. A tiny amount of dog meat is shredded into strips and is submerged in the soup.

Through a translator, the servers reassure us that it is *wild* dog. No *consommé* de lapdog will be served! As if it would make any difference.

I try one bite and it is chewy, a bit like beef, but gamey and not very good. When the second spoon brings up a little bone I start feeling nauseous and seek consolation in fluorescent kimchi.

CHAPTER SIX

EXPAT SLAVES

The hotel room has a fridge, a cupboard and a TV set all stowed away against the wall on one side. Blankets are piled on top, leaving only just enough floor space for the two mattresses. From my research I deduct that this is the typical set-up of an average house in North Korea. There is of course nil chance of us being shown one.

Officially, private-property ownership doesn't exist. Buying and selling property is illegal: all housing is allocated by the state and people live there for life. A token rent was introduced after 2002 and you are not allowed to move without permission. You are supposed to live near your place of work, and if you have a good reason to change residence (e.g. your parents are ill and you want to be near them) you can ask for a transfer. But with this, as with most other things in North Korea, the diktat has little to do with the reality on the ground. There is a buoyant property market in North Korea. People started to sell their homes during the famine, usually to buy food; some became homeless by doing so. Others sold their home to have cash to flee the country.

How are house sales achieved? If you can make do with a smaller house or a place less well-located, you can find a 'swapper' and swap his house for yours. Swapping is legal, as long as it is in the same county or city. That person pays you whatever is agreed in cash, and then the transfer is regularised by bribing both the housing guidance official and the housing unit manager to obtain the Certificate of Approval to occupy the unit.

You can go one step further: even if you don't have a house to swap, you can buy one. You may, for example, not want to wait until one is allocated to you, but the waiting lists are long. For newlyweds it can take years before they are allocated a house. Brokers with lists of houses for sale can be found in the 'illegal' private markets between the fruit and veg stalls. Again, the housing officials are simply bribed to issue or modify residency documents. It is even possible to develop land and build houses or blocks of flats provided the right people are bribed. A private developer can, for example, bribe an army officer to instruct soldiers to do the actual building of the apartment complex. Sometimes money from foreign investors, e.g. Japanese Koreans or South Koreans, is used. An alternative to bribing is to let officials and their families stay in the hotel afterwards for free.

The property price is paid for in US dollars, Chinese renminbi or whatever is agreed. Desirable apartments in Mansudae, in Central Pyongyang (sometimes called 'Pyonghattan'), may sell for as much as $100,000. The pricing is based on different factors from in the West: with intermittent electricity, flats on high floors are less desirable as the lifts often don't work. In earlier high-rise developments there often was a lift-shaft provided, but no actual lift to go with it. Even if there is a lift, it often feels unsafe: maybe it swerves all over the place while going up or down, or not all the buttons work. Flats near the Chinese border, from where it may be easier to travel abroad and run a thriving smuggling business, are expensive.

People who have defected often send money to their family in North Korea to buy better homes. There are illegal private money channels to achieve this – private banks, of sorts.

A few months after my visit to North Korea, the dictatorship finally caught up with the North Koreans' desire for private property. New boundary rules and new rules relating to the maximum allowed size of private property were introduced. A family is now allowed to own 87m^2 of land. Only one steam bath is allowed per ten units. Of course, just as with everything in 21st-century North Korea, regulations are merely a tariff list for bribes. Wealthy North Koreans just buy several adjacent properties and cut out doors between them. As with most places where there is no rule of law and where there are no defined property laws, those who don't have money to bribe suffer most: the poor are now regularly expelled from their land without recourse to compensation to make way for new developments approved by bent state officials.

We go on a walk through the town. It's a first: we can barely believe it. Sadly our shadow group – the other group that does exactly the same trip as ours and is headed by the *Gruppenführerin* and her male *Undergruppenführer* – are joining us.

'You have to walk two by two, behind each other. Please do not slack,' she admonishes us, self-righteousness dripping from her moon-like bossy face.

How little she understands Westerners. We take great mirth in winding her up by wandering chaotically in all directions to take photos. When one of the Lithuanians starts telling us off for not walking in pairs, mimicking her bossy voice, some chuckle while others shriek with laughter.

It certainly is interesting. It's the same colourless world we saw yesterday: all is grey, with the exception of red flags and aggressive slogans. It is early morning and some dewy mist still trails about as Kaesongians cycle to work. None smile. How many have an empty stomach? How many months have they not been paid? When the economic woes started, people often remained unpaid for years, but it is illegal not to work, even if you have not been paid. The practice has often been called 'state-sponsored slavery'.

The North Korean government does not just force its people to work for free in the homeland: it also hires out their services abroad and pockets their wages. Many North Koreans do aspire to work abroad, however. To be selected, the candidate must (1) be a loyal party member; (2) have family in North Korea who act as hostages; and (3) must not have family abroad. Bribes are accepted at every stage of the selection.

It is estimated that almost 50,000 workers have been dispatched to forty countries, including China, Russia, Mongolia and many African countries. Perhaps the gentleman from Cameroon who I met yesterday in the lift who said that he was on a 'Peace Mission' was in fact a recruitment agent. Farming out their workers brings in about $2 billion for the dictatorship.

An estimated 3,000 North Koreans have been hired to build the infrastructure for the 2022 World Cup in Qatar. They are supposed to receive their money at the end of their three-year term. Defectors have stated that they sometimes received less than 10 per cent of their actual pay. Some receive nothing. Most don't have one single riyal while in Qatar and have to borrow if they want to buy cigarettes. As they work in the scorching heat and for much longer hours than other nationals, they are much appreciated by the local developers. One North Korean worker at a building site in Doha told the British *Guardian* newspaper that he was there 'to earn foreign currency for the nation'.

Thousands work for logging companies in Siberia. They are supposed to be paid something like $200 a month, but usually they remain penniless for months on end. The salary is paid to a North Korean company; and here too, the worker will see only part of it. A normal working day is at least twelve hours, with two days off per year. They work in all weather. Some North Korean essentials brighten the camps, for example, statues of the Great Leaders. The administrative office is called 'Laboratory of Kim Il-sung Theory' to make them feel it is a home away from home. Many North Koreans have escaped from the logging sites and live illegally in Russia, permanently in fear of being deported.

When a North Korean died in a work accident in a shipyard in Gdynia (Poland), investigative journalists discovered that there are thousands of North Koreans working both legally and illegally in

Polish shipyards, factories, construction sites and agriculture. The company that employs them pays the wages to an agency, which in turn pays the Rungrado General Trading Company. This company is owned by the Workers' Party of Korea (Rungrado has a side-line exporting scud missile components to the Middle East). The workers receive their salary only when they return to North Korea five years later. They don't know how much that will be, as costs for clothing and facilities are deducted (as well as Rungrado's cut, of course). In Poland the North Korean workers labour about sixty hours a week; do not receive pocket money; do not enjoy holidays; are forced to live in isolated compounds; and are supervised by North Korean minders. Many are not allowed to keep mobile phones. The few who have escaped and applied for political asylum saw their family members back home thrown into concentration camps. According to the International Labour Organisation, the deprivation of wages, excessive working hours, threats of punishment and being forced to live in isolation constitutes slavery. The United Nations has labelled the practice 'forced labour'. Companies employing North Korean workers in the EU have received EU Development Funding of 70 million euros.

And the poor North Korean shipbuilder who died from a labour accident on that shipyard in Gdynia? His body was sent back to North Korea and his family received 636 euros in compensation.

As grim as it looks, even Kaesong has potential: some houses are old and beautiful, with pagoda-style roofs. But everything conspires against happiness: the absence of commercial sparkle, the unsmiling faces, the starkness of life. Unlike Pyongyang, we see no glitzy new buildings at all.

At the roundabout, loudspeakers harangue the cyclists. There are more boards with slogans and many more red flags. In the middle stands the Namdaemun, the old south gate of the walled city of Kaesong. What we see is a 1954 reconstruction. The original was built at the end of the fourteenth century at the time of the Kingdom of Koryo. The stone base has a tiny, rounded opening where traffic used to pass through, and an elegant, wooden pagoda on top. Little North Korean and red flags dangle from ropes that connect different sides of the roundabout with the roof. Mrs Kim braves the traffic and runs to the traffic island, to see whether we can enter. Unfortunately, the door is locked.

'You are stupid,' the gloating *Gruppenführerin* informs her in English when she returns.

Mrs Kim purses her lips.

'Don't lag behind,' the *Undergruppenführer* shouts at us.

Our minders decide that this 200m walkabout is quite enough excitement for today. We are corralled back onto the bus.

The Demilitarized Zone of Panmunjom lays 10km east of Kaesong.

'Please do not take any photos unless you are expressly permitted to do so,' Mrs Kim warns. 'Once you are in the DMZ your lives will be in the hands of the soldiers, and there is nothing we can do for you if it goes wrong!'

Mr Chong, for once, feels the need to add to this: 'I am a particular fan of the quote, when in Rome … oh, what was it…?' He looks puzzled. 'Oh, I have it. Do what you do as a Roman.'

We arrive just outside the gate that leads into the DMZ, and are shepherded into a single-storey concrete building with one more shop where you can buy posters in the socialist realism style, along with the jottings of the Kims in four languages and mud-coloured pottery. One in our group annoys me by buying and wearing a replica of a green 1960s Chairman Mao-style army cap with a red star. Does he have any idea how many people were killed by communist militia wearing those?

In an adjacent room, a soldier with an impressive kepi points out the different military landmarks on a wall-sized map of the DMZ. The DMZ is a strip of land of 2km on either side of the 1953 border, which runs along the Thirty-Eighth Parallel, but at an angle: south of it in the west, and north of it in the east. The maritime border was never agreed, so that creates permanent shenanigans. The DMZ divides Korea roughly in two halves. It's the buffer zone. Even though it is called 'demilitarized', it is one of the most heavily armed areas in the world. The Armistice Agreement stipulates precisely how many military personnel and which weapons are allowed inside the zone. Approximately 800 people have been killed there in 'incidents' over the years. A large number of tunnels were dug under it to help North Korea to invade the South, but most were detected. On the South Korean side you can visit them.

We are hurried out of the concrete building and then have to walk in a single line through a gate into the DMZ. I can think of no other reason for walking in this peculiar fashion than that our faces are filmed by a hidden camera. Our empty coach already drove in, and is waiting on the other side. It will deposit us 2km further at the border.

'No photos, please!' Mrs. Kim says again.

We are told the strip of land is mined; but bizarrely it is cultivated as well, and there are farmers about. We halt at a group of three perfectly maintained white buildings with blue window frames and a manicured garden with flowering cherry trees and topiary. This is where the village of Panmunjom used to be before it was flattened. A very handsome soldier with an impressive kepi will now be our minder. The invented history lesson is about to start.

First we visit a pleasant building with a large table in the middle where the Korean War peace negotiations took place.

'Because the American imperialists did not want peace, the negotiations took two years,' the pretty soldier sneers.

The reality was slightly different. Subject to heavy bombing from the United Nations army, Kim Il-sung feared that he would inherit a wasteland. By June 1951 he was eager to end the war. Mao, who used the Korean War to blackmail the Soviet Union into building armament factories in China and in order to safeguard China's territorial integrity, refused the request. He was quite happy to use China's almost inexhaustible manpower to tire out the enemy. The 'Human Wave Tactic' was used: during battles, wave after wave of dispensable soldiers were thrown in, until the enemy was overrun. Stalin didn't desire peace either, as he wanted China to keep the USA busy for a while longer, so he could achieve his goals elsewhere. For public relations reasons the USSR and China publicly declared they wanted peace. On 10 July 1951, negotiations were started in tents near the village of Panmunjom where we are standing now. Agreement was reached very quickly, but then Mao put his foot down on the 'tiny little issue' of the 21,500 North Korean and Chinese prisoners of war who were in the hands of the United Nations.

Most of the soldiers caught by the United Nations army were ex-Chiang Kai-shek soldiers who had previously surrendered to Mao and who Mao now enthusiastically used as cannon-fodder. Mao wanted them all returned to the People's Republic or North Korea. The United States refused this: they remembered how Stalin had ordered his soldiers to fight to the last man; and how those who surrendered had been declared deserters and sent to the gulag when they were returned by the West to the Soviet Union after the war.

The United States now wanted to send the Chinese and North Korean POWs back only *if they themselves agreed to return.* The stalemate resulted in the negotiations being in recess for another twenty-four months.

When the new US President Eisenhower announced that he was willing to use nuclear bombs against China, Mao asked Stalin for the atom bomb in return. Stalin didn't trust Mao with this toy and decided to end the war. He died on the same evening he took that decision. The new Soviet government disowned Stalin and wanted to thaw relations with the West. They ordered Mao to end the war. The Armistice between North Korea, the People's Republic of China and the United Nations was signed on 27 July 1953. About 1.1 million people, both civilian and military, had died.

Two-thirds of the POWs in the hands of the United Nations refused to go home and most settled in Taiwan. North Korea sent back 13,000 POWs. Tens of thousands of other South Korean prisoners held by North Korea were loaded onto lorries in Pyongyang. They thought they were going home to South Korea, but were carted off to new prisoner-of-war camps in the Hamgyeong-do and Jagang-do provinces on the border with China. During their detention, POWs had been housed in insanitary huts where they were not allowed to brush their teeth or wash themselves. After they were 'resettled' they ended the rest of their lives in similar abject circumstances. When they died their bodies were dumped in mass graves.

Hundreds of thousands of wealthy, educated and religious North Koreans used the end of the war as an opportunity to flee to South Korea, thereby sucking the life out of a possible opposition to the communists in Pyongyang that could have arisen.

For the signing of the Armistice a building was constructed in forty-eight hours by both sides working together: the North Koreans provided the labour; the United Nations Command provided supplies, generators and light to allow the work to continue day and night. The pretty soldier tells us this is the building we are now entering. Actually, it isn't: the original construction was in wood, and this one, built of stone or concrete, must be a replica. It is very large; the three tables that were used at the peace armistice signing ceremony seem minute in the cavernous space.

'On the date of the signing, at the very last moment, the United States switched the flag of the United States for a United Nations flag, to deny responsibility for the war,' the pretty soldier explains with self-righteous indignation. The once-coloured UN flag, now a tattered rag the colour of clay, is kept in a thumbed glass box. He does not mention that on his side the signatories were both China and North Korea.

We all have photos taken with the tattered flag, and I smile the pretty soldier into a joint photo. He likes the idea and asks through an interpreter whether I ran the marathon.

'No, I say. I did not.'

He keeps smiling and feels my biceps.

'But you are strong and well-built. You could have run it. Next time no photo if you do not run the marathon!'

We laugh.

Is he coming on to me?

On the walls are more 'exhibits' that 'prove' how the American imperialists committed genocide etc. And there are cameras, everywhere. 'They' are keeping a close eye on the visitors to this Museum.

We drive to the Joint Security Area. Our pretty soldier gives us some last instructions in front of a huge granite slab featuring Kim Il-sung's signature. The memorial stones must have been produced by the dozen because we see them everywhere.

Both North and South Korea have large visitors' buildings opposite each other, but South Korea's Freedom House, built in 1998, looks hipper and larger than North Korea's Panmun Hall. Freedom House was to be used by the Red Cross to host reunions of families separated since 1953. From these buildings, just 100m apart, tourists can stare at each other across the border.

We observe the surroundings from the second-floor terrace of Panmun Hall. At ground level half-way between the two buildings are seven windowless bungalows. The ones painted sky-blue have been built by South Korea; the North Korean ones are painted grey. These are nicknamed 'Conference Row', since the Military Demarcation Line is marked by a wire that runs across the roofs, in the middle. All negotiations since 1953 have taken place inside these buildings. We are not allowed inside them, but I have seen photos. They have rectangular barrack-style spaces and in the middle of each stands a table, and the border runs right through it.

On the North Korean side, a megaphone on a pole shouts at the soldiers on the other side. It must be annoying for the North Korean squaddies, too. Presumably neither side is allowed to use earplugs as they need to stay alert. Both sides have been carrying out nuisance broadcasts since 1953.

There was an incident on Sunday 16 November 1986 that remains unexplained to this day. At 12.50 p.m., all along the DMZ, North Korean loudspeakers announced that Kim Il-sung had died. Inside North Korea nothing similar was announced. Flags near the border were flown at half-mast. Never quite sure what North Korean outrage will leap across the border next, South Korea promptly put its police and army on the highest state of alert. The broadcasts went on for two days: wailing laments of the Sun of Korea's death interspersed with funeral music. On the Tuesday the messages from the loudspeakers became dissonant:

- 1.25 a.m.: 'Respected Comrade Kim Jong-il is the Eternal Leader of the nation'
- 3.30 a.m.: 'We will feel even greater happiness under his son Kim Jong-il'

- 6 a.m.: 'Vice Marshal O Chin-u has taken power and the people support him'
- 8.45 a.m.: 'Do not believe the rumours that Kim Il-sung is dead'
- 10.04 a.m.: 'The Star of the Nation has fallen'.

Then the broadcasts suddenly died. Nobody has ever been able to explain this strange incident. Was it an attempt to see how South Korea would react in the case of Kim's death? Or was there a coup attempt by North Korea's top brass? Vice Marshal O Chin-u did not suffer for having been declared Kim's successor: he was promoted to Marshal.

The nuisance broadcasts were suspended between 2004 and 2015. They resumed when two South Korean soldiers were wounded on the south side while stepping on land-mines laid by North Koreans. After four days of negotiations, North Korea expressed 'regret' for the incident, and the broadcasts stopped. South Korea then resumed them in January 2016 in response to the North's alleged testing of a hydrogen bomb, and North Korea followed suit. While we are here, the South Korean broadcasters must have the day off. Nobody needs to despair about the silence though: South Korea has promised that it will upgrade its loudspeaker system later this year.

We see unsmiling soldiers from the UN and South Korea on the other side standing still and glaring at us. We wave at the visitors on the other side who don't wave back: we are told by our pretty soldier that they are not allowed to do that. Australian Pete, who has been on the other side, confirms that they were indeed told not to wave back, for fear that North Korea would use those images in its propaganda films.

We hang around for ages. What I didn't observe at the time and heard only later is that virtually everybody else in my group uses this moment to send text messages to their loved ones across the world using the South Korean mobile phone network.

What a weird, weird place this is. Just like the centre of a cyclone, it feels bizarrely calm. All the North Korean soldiers have been smiling and make an easy-going impression. Their duties seem as untaxing as their numbers are derisory. A few weeks ago Kim III announced again that he was about to obliterate South Korea, but here it feels as if we are in a sleepy provincial town. Come to think of it, if the countries were really on the brink of war, they would not let tourists in this zone or anywhere near it. We are the proverbial canaries in the cage.

The only pre-communist architecture we are allowed to visit during our trip is the Songgyungwan compound. Being deprived of sun-bleached carvings and windswept stones makes me feel tender to the past. I ask Mrs Kim why we are not shown more ancient buildings.

'They were all destroyed during the Korean War,' she says, lips pursed.

Pyongyang was allegedly wiped off the face of the earth by 280,000 bombs. I rather suspect that quite a few old treasures met the sledgehammer after that. Invented history makes time start with the Kims, and no contradicting evidence is condoned: just as is the case in *Brave New World* in which there was a 'campaign against the past, during which historical monuments were blown up'.

The Songgyungwan compound was the main school at the time of the Koryo Dynasty (918–1392) which taught Confucianism: the same Confucius who believed in the 'Mandate of Heaven' and who believed that the populace was too stupid to make decisions themselves or elect their own leaders. The Kims must be his greatest fans. The buildings here were not only used as a school, but also as temples to perform the Confucian rites.

A minder in national hoop-dress and regulation socialist perm is beaming at us. The complex is a number of progressing walled squares; each one or two steps higher than the previous one. Each square has either a central building, or a central building with side annexes. All are single-storey, and are constructed in traditional wood and stone. They have pagoda-style roofs with beautiful old tiles. The complex definitely reminds me of Japan. The walls have very wide white grout, which means that the dark grey stones are like pretty islands dotted in a white sea. The portals in between the squares are in simple dark wood. The squares have a few strategically placed pine trees for decorative purposes.

The buildings house the Koryo Museum. There are allegedly more than 1,000 relics on display, but all of the buildings apart from the one on the square in the back are shut.

We see just one long room with a few maquettes, some maps, a number of old-fashioned glass display cabinets and large text explanations on the walls. For some reason the official minder rushes us through. She reels off the invented history of a number of sites and artefacts: pre-Kim time was all about evil, feudal landlords and courageous peasants' revolts, apparently. I cannot help but feel that the peasants were probably better off then than they are now.

The Koreans claim to be the inventors of both metal objects, and gunpowder. The other things I remember from the one-room museum are a number of rather beautiful but boring celadon vases elegantly decorated with little white storks; heaps of farmers' tools; a marvellous stone sarcophagus; and the reconstructed tomb chamber of King Kongmin with wall paintings that look very fine even in the prevailing gloom. One handy cartoon on the wall shows how in ancient times a cow was more expensive than a slave.

I am reprimanded for lagging behind and we are moved to the shop, which sells the works of the Kims and mud-coloured pottery. I have finally realised that the mud-coloured pottery is celadon! Celadon can refer to ceramics glazed in the green celadon colour ('greenware'), the colour celadon itself, and to the transparent glaze, often with small cracks (called 'crazing'), used on porcelain. The technique was invented in China, and fanned out into Thailand, Korea and Japan. The green colour comes in all sorts of hues and is meant to imitate jade. The correct green colour is obtained by firing a glaze that contains exactly the right dose of iron oxide. The Chinese Imperial court loved celadon, before blue and white porcelain pushed it from its pedestal.

I borrow fifty dollars from Australian Pete and buy the most beautiful object in the shop: an incense-burner featuring a rather frightful lion. I am proud to say that I saw him nowhere else. As lions go, he is one fine specimen.

Outside the museum hangs a red banner with a slogan ending with an exclamation mark.

'Let us all become honorary victors in the 70-Day Campaign of Loyalty!' Mrs Kim translates.

'In the run-up to the 7th Party Congress, Kim Jong-un urges all people in the DPRK to work extra hard for the country.'

Earlier I saw an article about this in the *Rodong Sinmun*, the mouthpiece of the Workers' Party of Korea. Titled 'Let's win the victory in the 70-day battle', it stated that 'revolutions proceed more powerfully in severe times, rather than in peaceful days'. Thermonuclear war would, it seems, be just the thing to advance the cause of the workers. The Politburo of the Workers' Party urges its members to join enthusiastically in the campaign because 'under current conditions when US imperialism and its lackeys are desperate to squeeze our socialist system, the devotion of all party members is a protest boasting of our strength'.

Campaigns like this used to be a regular feature in the former socialist countries, but only in North Korea they have survived. There is always some great event, sometimes as many as 100 days away, which warrants the long-suffering population being frog-marched into extra hard labour. During these campaigns, office workers will typically be told to help at building sites or in the fields after their normal working day is over. Sometimes the hours are so long that the workers have to sleep in the factories. According to the regime, backbreaking work is a great plus: Kim Jong-un wants to 'wipe out the evils of indolence and slackness'. Production targets must be exceeded! The imperative of heightened activity often proves a bit tricky with large numbers of factories shut because they lack electricity, spare parts or raw materials.

'The banners are there to remind people,' Mrs Kim adds helpfully.

'So will the 7th Party Congress take place at the end of the seventy-day period?'

'I don't know. The date for the 7th Party Congress has not been set yet.'

'And when was the 6th Party Congress?'

'In 1980.'

We move on to another subject.

I know that the actual tombs of the fourteenth-century King Kongmin and his queen are in the vicinity, but Mrs Kim says that we will visit the stamp shop instead, as those who went on the helicopter flight have not had the opportunity to buy stamps and cards. So there we are again in a grey room with shrill, neon-tube lighting where stamps and the works of the Kims are sold. They also sell socialist realism posters for such an exorbitant price that I double-check whether they are perhaps one-off signed original masterworks in transit to Sotheby's in New York: but nope, they are just posters. The shop also sells the usual ludicrous postcards. One shows a drawing of an expansive lunar base. Perhaps the government tells its people that they operate such a wonder? After all I've seen here already, this could easily be just a run-of-the-mill thought.

I do wonder whether my postcards will arrive in Blighty. I write nothing but high praise for the country, of course. I'm not sure if those employed at the Kim Il-sung letter-reading department 'get' the concept of irony. Incidentally: all the cards did arrive; some within a week, others within three months. Why the difference? Perhaps some scribblings had been escalated to a higher level in the department? In North Korea fact is usually stranger than fiction.

We drive in a north-eastern direction, back to the border, this time to observe 'the wall built by the American imperialists' from the observation trench. First we receive another lecture from a retired major-general with an impressive kepi and even more impressive rows of medal ribbons. Our single armchairs are positioned with their backs to the two opposite walls, and the Great Leaders are watching us from above. The general teaches the North Korean invented history relating to the DMZ all over again, and with great enthusiasm. We are too stupefied by the nonsense we hear to utter any views of our own, though I can see that especially American Tasha feels uncomfortable. I am annoyed when the others partake in the required clapping at the end of the fabrications.

We make a short 200m walk through a trench. Is the trench there to protect us from American imperialist snipers?

I never actually see the wall. Three strong binoculars stand ready, aimed at the border.

'The wall cuts 220 rivers off!' Mrs Kim states, anger flashing in her eyes.

'It perpetuates the evil division,' the major-general adds, full of self-righteous indignation. 'It is like cutting our blood off.'

I search and search but still I can't find the cursed wall. The only thing I see is a watchtower and a building with very large South Korean and United Nations flags. When I later ask American minder Josh whether he saw the wall, he looks as if I am somehow asking him a trick question. The South Koreans do not admit to the wall's existence; they do however admit that they built an anti-tank barrier.

The alleged wall is serious stuff down here. It is seen as a propaganda coup. Isn't it evidence that the American imperialists and their lackeys want to prevent Korea from being reunited?

Now the haranguing comes from the other side! Loudspeakers are blaring out … 'Delilah' by Tom Jones. It is absolutely surreal.

When we ask the general to pose for photos with us, he complains that everybody always promises to send him the photos afterwards, but that nobody ever does. British Paul promptly produces his Polaroid camera and now the general is very pleased indeed. I notice that behind our minders' backs the others are sending text messages again, using the South Korean network.

The three-hour drive back to Pyongyang is tedious. The problem with a group tour is that the time is never your own; you can never decide that you want to do something else, or, as is the case now: nothing at all. Every five years I go on a group tour to remind myself how much I hate the formula. Then again, however, it's a pretty good idea to travel to North Korea in a group as you meet far more people than on an individualised tour; your fellow travellers are a support network in case of trouble, and they can distract the minders while you take illegal photos.

Through the coach's side window I suddenly notice the elegant onion-domes of an Orthodox church. There are five of them, all in gold; the rest of the church is painted white and light-blue.

Mrs Kim is sitting next to me, and sees me stare. 'Yes, you see, there are churches in North Korea. People are allowed to go there. Do you want to go on Sunday? We can bring you.'

For a few seconds I'm speechless. In this country people are shot for owning a Bible.

I turn back to look at it some more. A 2m-high wooden palisade is skirting the church, and I can see no door.

'Yes, foreign propaganda media often say that religion is not allowed in North Korea. Religion is allowed, though nowadays only a few old people go to church. No young people. And we can bring tourists if they want. But they cannot preach or bring Bibles.' Does it sound confused even to her?

It is, of course, not as easy-going as Mrs Kim lets on. When he took power, Kim Il-sung had all Christian churches and most Buddhist temples flattened. Priests and other religious leaders were killed or disappeared. Only about sixty out of 400 Buddhist temples survive; 1,600 nuns and monks and 35,000 Buddhists have disappeared; 1,500 Protestant churches and their 300,000 followers have disappeared; three Catholic dioceses and 50,000 Catholics have disappeared; 120,000 followers of Chondoism have disappeared (Chondoism is Confucianised local shamanism). Kim Il-sung explained why and how the clean-up was achieved in a 1962 speech:

We cannot carry such religiously active people along our march toward a communist society. Therefore, we have tried and executed all religious leaders higher than a deacon in the Catholic and Protestant churches. Among other religiously active people, those deemed malignant were all put to trial. Among ordinary religious believers, those who recanted were given jobs; while those who did not were held in prison camps.

It is mainly the fear of alternative centres of power and the possible distraction from fidelity to Kim and the Juche ideology that steers this ecclesiophobia. In the Soviet-drafted North Korean Constitution, religion is separate from the state; there is religious pluralism and no religion is discriminated against. Religion is organised through a number of groups such as the Christian Federation, the Buddhist League, the Catholic Association, the Orthodox Committee and the Chongdokyo Central Committee. They fall under the umbrella of the Religious Practitioners Association. It is impossible to figure out whether these organisations are working concerns.

One should not be deceived by the hallowed phrases of the North Korean Constitution. In fact, the Constitution and the Workers' Party of Korea are subject to a higher order. First of all, the utterances of the three Kims, which have supra-legal power. Their word is law. Secondly, the constitution is subject to the Ten Principles of Unitary Ideology, which, from 1974 onwards, cemented the dictatorship and deification of the Kims and sought to organise all aspects of daily life for North Koreans. It states that 'everyone must firmly struggle against factionalism, parochialism, paternalism and other anti-Party elements, as well as day-dreaming and honey-chasing behaviours and eliminate all influence-peddling'.

These woolly sentences cover any behaviour disapproved of by the dictatorship. Religion is most certainly one of those.

The Orthodox church I see in Pyongyang is not unique. From 2000 onwards, the dictatorship allowed some South Korean religious groups to help fund the renovation of religious buildings, and even the building of a few new ones. Buildings with crosses on the roof can be seen in the the Mangyongdae district in Pyongyang. There are no Christian or Protestant churches outside of Pyongyang. No North Korean would ever contemplate worshipping in a religious building. Entry is limited to North Korean security service operatives and to foreigners only. North Koreans who wander in innocently are sent away to concentration camps. In fact, no interviewed defector was ever aware of the existence of operative churches.

When foreigners are brought in to visit, a carefully orchestrated charade is put on. Priests conduct religious rites and a few choice forty- to fifty-year-old operatives are planted in the pews, singing hymns etc. One group of tourists who asked to stop impromptu at a church on Easter Sunday found it duly locked. North Korea has sent a few of its citizens to Russia to study Orthodox Christianity, and a handful have even been ordained. Religion is also a course subject at Kim Il-sung University. Some officials are essentially taught to conduct religious services to cater to foreign visitors.

North Korea teaches its population that religion is superstition and a drug. He who is caught performing a religious act, such as possessing a Bible or saying grace at the dinner table, is sent to a concentration camp. Since 1997, North Koreans have received training in how to detect people proselytising Christianity. The 1981 *Modern Korean Dictionary* contains the following gems:

Christianity: conceals and legitimises the abuse and inequality of previous eras and uses the ridiculous idea of heaven to persuade people to obey the ruling class

Church: a place where poisonous anti-revolutionary ideology is used to abuse people under the mask of religion

Bible: a book about the fictitious and deceitful religious doctrine of Christianity

So why does the North Korean dictatorship bother with the 'we have churches' charade? If there is a firm policy behind it, what is it? First of all, so-called churches can placate gullible foreigners and foreign leaders. Since 1997, a number of joint religious ceremonies have been held between Catholic, Protestant, Orthodox and Buddhist groups from south and north of the border. These seem to serve a reputational and diplomatic purpose rather than a religious one. Secondly, it helps the secret police to catch innocent North Korean worshippers – a sort of 'cross-trap'. There are reported incidents of North Koreans venturing into churches and being arrested. And last but not least, through its different church organisations, the dictatorship can capture aid donations from foreign religious groups. During the famine, North Korean religious organisations made concerted efforts to contact their Western counterparts to ask for aid. The Unification Church of the Reverend Moon, for example, gives substantial aid to North Korea – and enjoys business interests there.

Large parts of the population go to fortune tellers. This is officially illegal, but the enforcers do it too.

The long day grows longer. It's dark already and we walk into yet another building that looks like an ordinary apartment block from the outside. On the third floor there happens to be a European-style bar with home-brewed beer. This is the famous Taedonggang, named after the Taedong River. The equipment used to make the beer came from a now-defunct British brewery. By size the bar looks more like a German beer hall; it even has varnished wood on the walls, and photos of alpine chalets and meadows in tacky frames.

North Korea is quite good at beer making. It is said that they have more breweries than South Korea. They were set up by the Japanese in the colonial era.

North Koreans are heavy drinkers and enjoy strong spirits. In many villages beer is considered a soft drink, which is also given to children. The dictatorship is quite happy to keep the population drunk and pliant with lax drinking laws. North Koreans drink alcohol in restaurants if they can afford it; or buy it illegally in the private markets. If they know somebody who works there, they can buy it directly from a brewery.

Alcohol is split into two categories: Number One, which is made only for the ruling Kim; and Number Two, for everybody else. Officially one cannot obtain Number One, but it can of course be bought on the black market. Needless to say, Number One gives you less of a headache than Number Two. Number One has the best taste and is made from potatoes. Traditionally, it was only permitted to drink domestically produced alcohol; nowadays you can also buy foreign alcohol in the market. The most popular drink is Kaoliang from China, which has up to 50 per cent alcohol content.

Most North Koreans can afford only brewery-produced alcohol on very special occasions. Most ordinary people stick to a home-made brew called *nongtaegi*, which is made from ginseng, rice, fruit or corn left to ferment in a bottle kept in a warm place, such as on a heated floor covered with a blanket. When the malt forms, it is mixed with warm water and left to ferment. It is then heated and when it starts boiling, the liquor is produced. Home distilleries are illegal, but everybody does it. The star private producers make a killing on the private markets. Kim II preferred the best cognacs, and Kim III is keen on exclusive red wines.

The six beers here at Taedonggang are numbered one to six, with number one being ordinary beer, six being beer made from rice, and the others mixtures of different percentages. I am the only one in the group who tastes beer made exclusively from rice. It tastes pretty much the same as ordinary lager, though those who taste from my glass are adamant that it is very different.

The event of the day is not the beer, but our first experience of a power cut! There we are in the dark, relishing the blackout failure, trying to take photos (or not). All of the books and articles we've consulted before we came here mentioned the many power cuts. The travel agency's guidance notes advised us to bring a torch. And now, here it is: the real thing. We clink to it, and then the neon tubes flicker on again.

In the 1990s North Korea produced only one fifth of the electricity it needed. Even that shortage was misallocated as party bigwigs issued clashing orders to prioritise their personal supply. Today, a person's rank in the system can be ascertained by finding out whether he enjoys 24-hour electricity supply or not. Even in the diplomatic quarter, electric appliances malfunction because of insufficient voltage.

The regime takes power cuts in Pyongyang very seriously and even more so when they happen during official festivities. In January 2012 four people working at the Jangjin River Power Plant in South Hamgyong Province were executed for mishandling the power supply to Pyongyang and causing a blackout on Kim Jong-un's birthday (which is called the 'Day of the Sun').

When you see the Korean peninsula from space, the North is completely in the dark, while the South is lit up like a Christmas tree. In many villages electricity is intermittent, and sometimes the houses go without it for days on end. This also means that the water doesn't run, and that lifts in high-rise apartment blocks don't work. Many people light their flats with kerosene lamps instead. The monuments to the Kims are, of course, always brightly lit.

The dictatorship must have somehow increased the country's electricity supply since then, because we have not really noticed shortages. Unless, perhaps – and this we cannot check – the power supply to the north is switched off during the Pyongyang marathon when so many foreigners and foreign press are around in the south. It sounds more far-fetched than it is.

Kim Jong-un is determined to increase nuclear power. At the

moment, North Korea does not have electricity from nuclear power plants.

In the restaurant a few blocks down the road, we have to prepare our own food. We each have a small cooker with a bowl containing a simmering light broth. On the side is a microscopic plate with a few wilted greens and lacklustre salad that we can throw into the broth. The meat is coarse and the whole concoction tastes of nothing. It is called *chongol*, which means 'meat-and-vegetable hotpot'. We drink the complimentary bottle of beer to forget the food. The Lithuanians mischievously order something stronger and pour generously for our minder Mr Chong. His face goes red and he starts sweating profusely. He becomes unusually merry. Even though she had only one glass of beer, Mrs Kim seems a bit tipsy, too. On the bus home they both sing karaoke. Mrs Kim goes for the anodyne 'Nice to Meet You', but Mr Chong's Korean song sounds more revolutionary. We decide to get them drunk more often.

I'm annoyed: the bottle with the snake inside leaks. And it stinks. Thankfully it has drenched only the plastic bag inside my luggage I had put it in, so nothing else is ruined. Disheartened, I bin it at the Yanggakdo Hotel.

North Korean state enterprise has been producing primitive products that nobody wants for decades. Before, North Korea bartered its sub-standard merchandise with the other socialist countries in exchange for fuel, technology and consumer goods. North Korea was a useful ally for the socialist bloc: an outpost and buffer against the free world. Kim Il-sung used the geopolitical importance of his country to negotiate these uneven bargains: aid masqueraded as trade.

In the 1960s, North Korea was not doing too badly compared with South Korea: both were tyrannies. But the division had left North Korea with the heavy industrial infrastructure the Japanese had built there in the 1930s. Notwithstanding the bombing in the Korean War, many of these industries survived or were quickly repaired. With some reason, North Korea could claim that it had 'nothing to envy' from the outside world. The slogan was even printed on its banknotes and taken up in the lyrics of many patriotic songs, a bit like the slogan 'Our new, happy life' in *Nineteen Eighty-Four*.

When Eastern Europe and the Soviet Union introduced capitalism in the 1990s, their freshly privatised companies started demanding hard currency for the products, parts and raw materials North Korea needed. Nobody wanted North Korea's sub-standard goods any more. Today, the trade between Russia and North Korea is less than 5 per cent of what it used to be in Soviet times. China picked up the shortfall, and continues to support Pyongyang: trade with China has grown from 500 million dollars in the 1990s to 6.6 billion in 2013.

The cessation of inter-communist barter caused the collapse of the North Korean economy. Raw materials, fuel and parts could no longer be obtained. Factories and power stations stopped functioning and turned to rust. Often it was a vicious circle: North Korea is mineral rich, but all that could be mined with primitive technology had been mined already. More advanced machinery could not be bought abroad as there was no hard currency to pay for it; and it could not be produced at home as there was a lack of electricity. With frequent power cuts, factories could not function. Often the machines themselves were damaged because of the cuts. People were still obliged to go to work, but they had nothing to do and their salary stopped being paid. In North Korea all vital statistics are state secrets, but it is estimated that between 1990 and 2000 the GDP of North Korea halved. Between 1991 and 1995 the per capita annual income dropped from $2,460 to $719.

The economic crisis also had a devastating effect on agriculture, and was one of the causes of the famine. Dangerous pesticides and intensive farming had already damaged the soil. Now there was no money to buy fertilisers abroad and no fuel for the few tractors available. The North Korean leadership's obsession with self-reliance led to diktats for the state farms to grow crops for which the North Korean soil and climate are unsuitable.

CHAPTER SEVEN

ACCESS TO THIS INFORMATION IS TEMPORARILY UNAVAILABLE

Off to downtown Pyongyang again. The zig-zagging in and out of Pyongyang to assorted Sites of Outstanding Communist Interest has everything to do with prior approval from up high having to be obtained first. A tourist group cannot just turn up at a site. Also, a specific minder in a black velvet robe with diamanté sequins and regulation socialist perm must be allocated. At no point are we provided with an itinerary. My repeated requests for one receive the 'me not understand' treatment.

We are grouped in front of the most prominent building in Pyongyang: it is large and beautiful, and stands in prime position on Kim Il-sung Square. It is aligned with the Juche Tower and the Party Foundation Monument. At first I mistook it for the presidential palace.

'No,' Mrs Kim says, 'this is the Grand People's Study House. Thanks to our Great Leader Kim Il-sung, people can study and read books there.'

'I thought it was the president's palace! Where is the president's palace?'

She looks bewildered.

'Where does Kim III live and work? Where is his palace?'

She composes herself.

'Oh, no. President does not live in a palace. When we say palace we mean the Kumsusan Memorial Palace of the Sun, where the Great Leaders Kim Il-sung and Kim II's mausoleums are. We will go there on the last day. It is the highlight of the visit.' She looks eager to stop this silly line of questioning.

'But surely he must live somewhere? Is it in the centre of Pyongyang?'

There is annoyance in her voice. 'I don't know. Not in a palace. Perhaps in some house or something.' She turns around and waves to the group. 'Come on, hurry up. We have appointment!'

So the North Koreans don't even know where their Leader lives. I guess it's better to keep it secret, the leaders being so universally admired and all. Matt whispers in my ear: 'Perhaps they do it to keep the mystery going. So Kim Jong-un suddenly appears, as if having come down from heaven. A sort of apparition.'

Fortunately we now enjoy Google Earth. The North Korea Uncovered Project has revealed all: over a period of two years a doctoral student and volunteers studied images, books and news reports about North Korea. The end result was the most comprehensive map ever produced. The world now knows where in the sites of natural beauty the concentration camps are dotted about; what the entrance of the subterranean nuclear test site looks like; and where Kim Jong-un's fourteen palaces are located. The Ryongsong Palace in Pyongyang, for example, built during his grandfather's reign, is Kim Jong-un's main residence. The complex covers an area of 12km and has a nuclear bunker, several man-made lakes and an underground train station. It is connected to other palaces by way of tunnels. Kim Jong-il's Sinuiju palace looks vast, with copper-green pagoda roofs and its own private train station. The palace on Wonsan Bay houses the leader's private yachts, jet-skis and palaces for guests. The Kwangdong Palace, just outside Pyong-yang, is a summer residence. It is here that the Japanese chef Kenji Fujimoto famously stayed with Kim Jong-il.

Fujimoto was Kim's personal chef for eleven years. Initially, he had signed a one-year contract to teach Korean chefs how to make sushi. Four years later he was enticed back to become Kim's personal chef. It is through him that the world acquired a unique insight into what goes on behind the Kims' palace walls.

Fujimoto stayed in kitsch-filled marble palaces. He skilfully carved sashimi from live fish on yachts for Kim's closest generals, and rode the white stallions of Kim's stables. He also noticed how those close to Kim disappeared one by one.

He was in charge of satisfying Kim's every culinary whim. He dutifully flew to Beijing to pick up Big Macs; to Iran and Uzbeki-stan to source caviar; and to Denmark for ham. In France he was the purveyor of what has often been described in the evil capi-talist media as 'Kim's $700,000 cognac habit'. Kim Jong-il did not of course drink all those bottles himself; he handed them out to party cadres on Kim Il-sung's birthday, New Year's Day, and his own birthday. On the black market they sell for $100 or more each. The cadres will receive back many of the bottles they sold by way of bribes.

The Japanese chef became Kim's confidant: drinking claret together from Kim's 10,000-bottle wine cellar, discussing the intricacies of foie gras and kobe beef, playing baccarat and talking about life in Japan. Kim's favourite Schwarzenegger films were another regular topic. Fujimoto even met Kim's women (usually known as his sex-slaves). Beautiful girls used to be kidnapped from countries like Thailand, but as this received too much bad press, he picked North Korean girls instead. Section 5 of the Organisation and Guidance Department selects girls at the age of thirteen, around the time they start to menstruate. They are then checked annually, to ensure that they have no diseases and that they are still virgins. Age sixteen, a selection is made. The 'lucky' ones are given one year of training and are taken to one of the Kims' many palaces, where they sing, dance and provide whatever the Leader desires for himself and his friends. They are known as the *kippeumjo*, or 'joy division', and are forcibly kept locked up in the palaces, guarded by Kim's bodyguards. The bodyguards themselves are chosen from orphans so their only allegiance is to the Kims. The girls are dismissed at around the age of twenty-four; usually this is done by Kim ordering them to marry one of his cadres.

Fujimoto's career almost came to an end when he was arrested in Japan while buying sea urchins for Kim in 1996. The Japanese secret service was keen to catch him as the outside world knew next to nothing about Kim's private life. They questioned him for eighteen months before he was eventually released. He returned to North Korea, as he missed his wife and children, but he kept in touch with the Japanese police. When the North Koreans found out about this, he was put under house arrest for eighteen months. When he returned to Kim's inner circle, he realised how many people close to Kim had 'disappeared'. He escaped to Japan in 2001, but his North Korean wife and children were sent to a coal mine to be re-educated. He sent a letter of apology to Kim and they were freed after six years.

During his eleven years' stay in North Korea, Fujimoto also became young Kim Jong-un's playmate. He introduced him to remote-control cars, gaming and basketball. According to Fujimoto, young Kim drinks a lot, and easily downs two bottles of Cristal champagne in one sitting (the exclusive champagne in a crystal bottle that was first made for Russian Tsar Alexander II and easily costs £175 a bottle in the UK). Swiss-educated Jong-Un also has a bit of an addiction to Swiss Emmental cheese – something that goes some way towards explaining his expanding waistline. In his father's tradition, he sent officials to a French state-run dairy industry school (the École Nationale d'Industrie Laitière) to improve North Korea's cheese making. The College rejected the request 'as it did not fall within its priorities and strategy'. After Kim Jong-il died, Jong-un invited Fujimoto back to North Korea. There was a tearful reunion.

Going back to basketball, former NBA star Dennis Rodman described his visits to the Kims' palace and his stay on Kim's private island as a 'seven star party venue' with groups of about fifty or sixty people enjoying endless cocktails, jet-skiing and riding Kim's horses: 'When it's tequila, it's the best tequila. Everything is the best.' Rodman also described Kim's 60m yacht as a cross between a ferry and a Disney boat. Kim also owns a 30m Princess 95MY yacht that cost about $5 million and was produced by LVMH. He uses it to visit poor fishing villages in the coastal regions. Kim Jong-un owns at least one private jet (a Russian IL-62 jetliner) that looks similar to the American President's Air Force One (dubbed 'Air Force Un' by pranksters). Google Earth recently revealed that five neat little airfields were completed right next to a few of Kim's palaces to cater for his private jet.

Anyway, today we are not going for coffee chez Kim. The sheer size of the Grand People's Study House beggars belief. We meet in front of an oversized portrait of Kim Il-sung standing in a soft meadow of Kimilsungia, the purple orchid that carries his name. Unusually, our minder is not in national dress. Perhaps intellectuals (one third of the catchment population of the Workers' Party) escape the stricter sartorial guidelines to which the lesser North Koreans are subject.

'The Grand People's Study House was built in just twenty-one months to celebrate the Great Leader Kim Il-sung's seventieth birthday!' she shouts enthusiastically.

'Impossible,' Carlos, who builds public buildings in Colombia, susurrates through his teeth. 'The interior alone would take that time. It's complete nonsense. They would have to be the fastest builders in the world. They would be in charge of all the construction sites on the planet if it were true.'

'We have 30 million books. The Grand Study House covers 100,000m² and has more than 600 rooms!' she continues shouting.

'Mrs Kim, why is this building so empty? There is nobody here.'

'They are all preparing for the Leader's birthday.'

They must be sitting in a square somewhere waving wooden flowers in sync in front of an instructions-spitting megaphone.

We march to the central hall. It is perhaps 60m by 20m, and three floors high. Again, very few 'students' are hanging around. The library is aimed at people who want to study outside of the usual university or school environment.

'The Grand People's Study House allows North Koreans to receive further socialist training and to develop ever greater love and respect for the Great Leader and the Dear Leader! It is also an internationally revered centre for Juche study,' our minder shouts at the top of her voice. I'm surprised there is no echo.

'People come here to familiarise themselves with all aspects of Juche thought. Some spend more than one hour a day studying Juche!' This is on top of their lowly paid state jobs with compulsory attendance, the compulsory attendance at events organised by the organisations they are obliged to be a member of, and their moonlighting to try to earn enough to buy food on top of their insufficient rations: studying Juche one hour a day must be a big deal.

We cross a lofty corridor. I am intrigued by the arrow pointing the way to the 'Area of Education through Revolutionary Materials'.

We are herded into the 'Music Appreciation Room'. The Great Leaders are watching us. The room reminds me of the languages class in my school in the 1980s with its little wooden desks with privacy side panels to allow one to listen to music through bulky headphones with chunky spiral wires. The room supervisor switches on some American rock 'n' roll to prove that they have it. In North Korea it is illegal to share or enjoy foreign music unless it is specifically authorised by the authorities or if one is studying foreign music at university. It's not permitted to play, for example, The Beatles' 'Let It Be' on the home piano in front of friends.

In a room with about 100 chairs and desks, only four are occupied. Strangely, the students do not look up when the foreigners gather and make noise behind them.

Our minder points at the desks. 'When the Great Leader Kim Il-sung visited the Grand Study House for the first time he noticed how the taller students had to crouch over the low tables. So he invented these desks that have an adjustable height and incline!' Hong Kong Edward suppresses a giggle.

At the back, a table exhibits some goodies for sale: North Korean DVDs, some T-shirts and the Kims' writings. Most of the DVDs feature soldiers, missiles and tanks; but there are also some romantic flicks of the 'poor farmer boy meets poor farmer girl but they are persecuted by the evil landlord'-type. And some animation films for children featuring cuddly toys and tanks in sherbet colours; I shudder to think what the synopsis is.

Kim Jong-il was a film buff: North Korean diplomats abroad were tasked with sending him copies of the latest blockbusters. His favourites were the *Rambo* films, the James Bond films and anything with Elizabeth Taylor in it. He was rumoured to have the largest private film collection in the world. In 1973 he published a book called *On the Art of Cinema*. In the preface he imparted the paradigm-shifting insight that 'the cinema is now one of the main objects on which efforts should be concentrated in order to conduct the revolution in art and literature'.

Before he became dictator he ran the Ministry for Propaganda; and set about building a North Korean film industry. Eventually the Korean Feature Film Studio occupied 1 million square metres. The films usually have the same plots: individual = bad; self-sacrifice for the collective = good; South Koreans are degenerates and prostitutes and double up as lackeys of the American imperialists.

As Kim Jung-il thought the quality was somewhat lacking, he set up a James Bond-style covert operation to kidnap talent. In 1978, the famous South Korean actress Choi Eun-hee was lured to a meeting on one of Hong Kong's islands to talk about a possible appearance in a new film. En route, her car stopped at Repulse Bay. She was grabbed by a group of men, taken into a motor boat and sedated. She drifted in and out of consciousness. She remembers someone carrying her through a corridor, and somebody else giving her an injection. When she finally woke up she was in a cabin on a ship with a large portrait of Kim Il-sung grinning at her.

Her ex-husband, the famous film-maker Shin Sang-ok, travelled to Hong Kong to find her and was promptly abducted as well. Shin was put up in a North Korean palace, but for good form he was thrown in prison after two escape attempts. When his re-education was thought to have been successful he was brought before Kim, who commanded him to make films for him. He was also allowed to meet his wife, who, until then, had not known that he was in the country as well. Shin directed eight films while in North Korea, with Kim Jong-il giving on-the-spot guidance throughout. The most famous one, *Pulgasari*, became a cult classic: a monster film in which the monster sides with the peasants against an evil landlord. In 1986 husband and wife escaped while attending a film festival in Vienna, and received asylum from the USA before later moving back to South Korea. North Korea still produces a few films every year, but with the growth of imports from China and the realisation that North Korea cannot compete, it is nearly moribund. Sometimes defectors to North Korea are used as actors: a handful of American deserters from the Korean War have enjoyed a glittering career in North Korean films portraying evil American imperialists.

Kidnapping became a bit of a cottage industry in North Korea. Most instances we will never know about, but during the Korean War more than 84,000 civilian South Koreans were taken from their homes by North Korean and Chinese soldiers. They turned up with lists of who was to be taken and they mainly took intelligentsia.

A state policy even more sinister than that of kidnapping film-makers was the abduction of foreigners under the 1970s 'Localisation Project'. This was operated from Room 35, which housed the Foreign Investigations Bureau. Innocents were kidnapped and brought to North Korea to train as North Korean spies and to facilitate identity theft. The kidnapped were often forced to marry North Koreans or other foreigners in order to produce offspring who could be indoctrinated into becoming spies. They included citizens of Japan, Macao, Thailand, France, Italy, the Netherlands, Romania, Lebanon and Syria. They were usually forgotten; their governments did not take up their cases as the abduction theories seemed too fantastical to be believed. Four Lebanese women were freed in 1980 after their government intervened. They recounted how their passports were taken and how they were sent to indoctrination classes to turn them into firm adherents of Kim Il-sung. They said that there were twenty-eight young women at the centre, including three Italians, three French, two Dutch and many women from the Middle East.

The abductions of Japanese individuals and couples are well-documented. Japan officially believes there were seventeen abductions in the 1970s and 1980s. When attempting to extract US $11.4 billion of war reparations from Japan in 2002, Japanese Prime Minister Koizumi brought up the issue of the abductions during a summit in Pyongyang. Kim Jong-il begrudgingly admitted kidnapping thirteen, and mumbled an apology. This caused an explosion of outrage in the Asian media. North Korea allowed five to visit their homeland and said the others had died – something Japan does not believe. The five refused to return to North Korea. Kim Jong-il stamped his feet and said that there would be no further summits with Japan in his lifetime. There were probably many more kidnappings, possibly hundreds. Professor Andre Lankov of Kookmin University puts the number at more than 500 South Koreans in the past fifty years. These include lost South Korean operatives, and people who innocently strayed into North Korean territory. Occasionally there are sightings of disappeared citizens in North Korea.

In March 2015 the UN Human Rights Council strongly criticised North Korea after it found that up to 200,000 foreigners from at least twelve countries had been abducted (this included the South Koreans kept by North Korea after the war).

Inside the Grand Study House, they now proudly show us into a computer class. Chunky table-monitors are switched on and we are urged to do some searches. Internet use is strictly limited in North Korea: imagine if the prisoners heard about the world outside! One tourist claims that when he asked his guide why there was no internet, she replied that 'the government wants to protect the reputation of the West; to ensure that North Koreans would not be unfairly prejudiced against them.'

Only a few thousand North Koreans have access to the worldwide web: the political elites and their families, the country's cyber warfare agencies and some students at top universities. Their use is monitored. In 2014 North Korea banned satellite internet connections and Wi-Fi networks at foreign embassies, unless they have permission from the government. Before, North Koreans were able to access the web by hanging around embassies. There were even rumours that some had moved to apartments near embassies for that sole purpose. The measure came after the embassies had ignored requests from the government to reduce the strength of the Wi-Fi signals, or to block access by way of passwords. A few cheekily continued to beam out very strong signals. Some signals can be picked up near the Chinese border, but in China the internet is censored too so the North Korean government isn't too concerned. Foreign visitors to North Korea are able to access the internet and receive international phone calls by buying pre-paid SIM cards. When they left the country some naughty foreigners handed their cards to North Koreans, who could then use them – so Koryolink, the country's 3G mobile operator, began deactivating them on the last day of their visit.

The computers here in the Grand Study House are connected to the North Korean intranet called Kwangmyong. It contains a few thousand web pages, although most are stolen from the worldwide web and carefully censured and monitored.

Our Lithuanian techie uses our minder's momentary distraction to quickly type some keys, going straight for the code. An 'Access to this information is temporarily unavailable' message flashes up. He tries some other routes but the same message pops up again and again. With a wry smile, he gives up.

The next corridors are really dark: perhaps energy is being saved? We now enter the library book room. Behind a closed counter we see some shelves with some unloved-looking books, all bound in pale-yellow. One cannot just take a book off the shelf, as in the West: all books must first be searched in the catalogue, and must then be requested from the librarians.

All North Korean authors are employed by the state. You are allowed to write only if you are friendly to the regime and if you have been expressly commanded to write a specific book by the Workers' Party of Korea. When your manuscript is finished it must be approved by the censors before it will be admitted for printing.

It is not the job of an author to be original or to pen down his own ideas. All written work serves to expand on the great deeds of the dictator and to support the Juche ideology. Whereas under Kim Il-sung the regime encouraged novels, Kim Jong-il preferred shorter poetry – the main reason for this was the shortage of paper.

And what about foreign books? In the 1960s the regime made a big effort to destroy foreign books in private ownerships. This even included Soviet books, which, after Khrushchev came to power, were considered 'too liberal'. It is illegal for North Koreans to obtain foreign books. When they find one, they have to report it to the police. Books are smuggled in from abroad, and some read South Korean books saved as e-files on their phone. Illegal book rental shops also exist.

Some foreign books are translated into Korean, and embassies worldwide are tasked with sourcing what might be worthwhile translating. Many are produced under the 'One Hundred Copies Series': only 100 copies are produced in secret by the Propaganda and Agitation Department. The 100 books are then carefully distributed to high cadres, the secret service and some universities. Each book is numbered from one to 100 so each copy can be traced. Number One goes to number one, which means that you can fathom someone's ranking by how low the number in his book is. All foreign books here in the Grand Study House are firmly behind lock and key, and it requires strict security clearance to read them. This even applies to old copies of North Korean magazines and newspapers: the regime doesn't want people to find out what part of history has recently been rewritten, or who was purged.

North Koreans can attend lectures on a range of subjects at the Grand Study House. Retired professors often 'volunteer' for this, 'for free'.

We enter a large and mostly empty room where a drab woman in green uniform looks up, terrified, from behind her desk. Our minder explains who we are. She doesn't smile back.

'You can ask her any question,' Mrs Kim urges.

Is this woman some sort of oracle-in-residence? One or two of us ask something aseptic and receive robotic replies that are translated by Mrs Kim.

I quickly open a few drawers while she isn't looking. The filing cabinet is completely empty.

In the hall we finally bump into some students. This was unplanned: about a dozen smiling guys in their early thirties are just streaming out of an English class. One of the Lithuanians asks one of them whether he speaks Russian, but before he can answer, Mr Chong pulls the Lithuanian's sleeve and drags him away. Mr Chong can monitor our English, but not our Russian! The regime not only tries to keep out outside information by way of book, radio and TV censure, but also by reducing all contact between North Koreans and foreigners outside of their strict duty. North Koreans interacting with foreigners will suffer the consequences. In any event, very few North Koreans are taught English. Wanting to learn a foreign language is highly suspicious.

The few foreigners living in Pyongyang receive detailed instructions aimed at keeping them away from North Koreans: they are not allowed to visit people at home; they cannot attend classes with

North Koreans; and they cannot go to the cinema when North Koreans are present. Back home, Westerners who visited North Korea are often asked whether they managed to speak to ordinary North Koreans, and what they said.

Even if a North Korean dared to talk to a foreigner, he is likely to say very little of interest. Hoping that a North Korean will criticise the regime is completely laughable: why would he risk his family and himself being dragged off to a concentration camp by confiding in a complete stranger for three minutes?

In one of the main halls, four young students at a table wave at us enthusiastically and smile broadly. We are too flabbergasted to wave back. We follow our minder to the exit.

CHAPTER EIGHT

COOL KIDS WITH
MOLOTOV COCKTAILS

'The Pyongyang-Nampo Highway was built exactly 42km long to celebrate the forty-second year of our Great Leader Kim Il-sung coming to power,' Mrs Kim cheerfully cackles through the microphone.

'I do wonder how they managed to make the distance between two cities so precise: did they put in extra bends, or is it perhaps a bit too long or too short?' I ask Australian Pete, who sits next to me.

'You can't believe anything they say,' he replies.

Actually, it's 46.3km long.

'This road is sometimes called the Youth Hero Motorway, because of the youths who built it. They volunteered for this job,' Mrs Kim muses.

'Don't believe it,' Pete says. 'They just order the people to turn up to carry out all sorts of jobs. The authorities keep a written record of individuals' "volunteering", which follows them throughout their lives.'

To amuse Kim II, that well-known aesthete who loved the theatre, the construction of this road was turned into a comedy for the theatre. *Youth Shines* portrayed 'the lives of the merry youths mixed with tears of laughter and deep emotion'. I'm surprised it never came to the West End.

The road was finished in just two years and opened in 2000. With six lanes in each direction, it would be very impressive indeed, were it not for the fact that it doesn't appear to have been maintained since then. Our driver cunningly uses the fast lane even though the white lines separating them have long disappeared into potholes. The car suspension industry must be doing a brisk business. We are thrown up and down in our seats, but only we mind the state of the road as there is nobody else on it. Very occasionally we spot a cyclist who takes a pensive look at us. Picnickers or slackers enjoy their working day crouching by the side banks.

In the evening I hear how in the other group one of the guys has a fitness watch that measures the number of steps he does every day. To his surprise, it showed that today he had walked ten times more than the days before! His watch had counted bumps as steps.

We will visit the 'world-famous' West Sea Barrage (or Nampo Dam), of which no one of us has ever heard before. It has thirty-six sluices, allowing ships of 50,000 tons to get through. It closes off the western end of the Taedong River (which also flows through Pyongyang) from the Yellow Sea.

We drive through Nampo, another ugly industrial town. The entrance to the road covering the dam is shielded by two statues of the heroic worker type. There are no other cars. Many locals are making the 8km crossing on foot or by bicycle. The coach stops at the visitor centre on P'i Do Island.

The lecture room has kitschy single armchairs. We are offered tea or coffee. A bookcase at the end shows off the writings of the Kims. There are a number of framed quotes from Kim Senior. What to think of 'Books are treasure-house of knowledge and the textbooks for a person's life.' Genius, no? Such a shame most people are not allowed books except those written by the Kims.

The Kims themselves are watching us from their photos above the smallish television screen on which we are shown the video of the dam's construction. The voiceover is enthusiastic, and the turgid language is archaic and hilarious.

'The immortal leader Kim Il-sung came personally down many times and decided to build a dam at the present place for the everlasting prosperity of the fatherland,' it goes. A grainy black-and-white film of great antiquity shows Kim surrounded by speed-clapping workers. The cynosure has two soldiers in tow who diligently record his every sigh.

'The dam was constructed for the great fatherland to first prevent salt water from entering fresh water, thereby solving the water supply problem; and second, to create additional farmland to feed the farmers and workers!' Cranes are shown dumping concrete boulders and earth into a choppy sea.

'The workers and the soldiers said: 'Let us commit ourselves to national defence and socialist construction.' (I must say it sounds more rousing than 'let's have a tea break'.) Thousands of workers are shown crawling around in the mud. The momentum is kept up by way of an excited drum roll.

'Kim Jong-il came personally down many times to teach them procedure and methods of construction!' A still shows Kim II authoritatively pointing at a map, and workers looking spellbound.

'Soldiers of twenty years of age did dangerous construction under water!' Divers in 1950s diving suits (the year is 1981) are shown jumping into water with ice-plates floating on it. Foreign diplomats at the time reported that hundreds of young people had died in the process.

The heroic music reaches its apotheosis when the end product is shown.

'The dam was finished in 1986, after only five years. Experts, technicians and workers had come together in high yet sacrificing spirit!' Enthusiastic crowds are shown, including applauding Europeans who look slightly bemused, as well as a photo of Kim Jung-il, who, for some reason, is accompanied by President Carter.

I have the giggles throughout and frantically try to write down the hilarious voiceover verbatim. In reality, though, it is not that funny. The dam has been widely blamed for destroying vast plots of farmland, and thus contributing to the North Korean famine. It was built in only five years but the ramshackle construction started crumbling within weeks.

The film ends, and the minder waits expectantly for Johnny Foreigner to 'ooh' and 'ahh' over the achievement. We all look blank and nonplussed, not wanting to give her anything. She shrugs and leads us up the stairs to the viewing platform on the roof. As the whole area is covered in a dense white fog, we can't see a thing. We are all shivering, but are nonetheless left outside for about half an hour. When I go back into the building, I spot a framed poem in the corridor. It's the official Nampo Dam poem:

'O shine for all centuries to come;
Great monument of the 80s built
By our design, our technique, and our strength;
The great creation made in our own way.
Only a great leader
A great party can conceive the idea.
Only a great people can build you
West Sea Barrage, the world's greatest.
Rise high to symbolise the power of self-reliant Korea
And tell and retell the everlasting achievement
Of our Great Leader
Forever and ever and ever.'

Now we visit another exhibit that explains why North Korea went hungry. Our tour of the Chongsan-Ri Cooperative Farm starts at a 30m-long monument with text in Korean and images of Kim I, Kim II and Mrs Kim I (General Kim Jong-suk, about whom more later). There is also a separate mural of an amiable Kim Il-sung sitting on a straw mat with apple-cheeked farmers listening intently; bulging haystacks and modern farm machinery crowd the background.

'This is famous farm!' our new minder in floor-length black

velvet robe with diamanté sequins and regulation socialist perm announces. 'Here General Kim Il-sung taught the people how to farm and gave instructions for all cooperative farms in the country!' She sounds like a true believer.

'This monument is to commemorate that Kim Il-sung came here, saw the land and decided that this should be a cooperative farm!'

Like Moses seeing the Promised Land.

'Over there,' she points at a low, white building about 200m away, 'is the museum. It is there that General Kim Il-sung stayed for two weeks in 1960.'

Turning houses where the Great Leaders stayed for however short a period into shrines is a long-standing tradition of this country. In Chongjin, a house where the wife of Kim Il-sung lived for one month has been preserved for eternity and turned into a museum; in Pyongyang the house where Kim Il-sung wrote the 'Report to the Inaugural Congress of the Workers' Party of Korea' (which established the Party in 1945) was turned into a museum; and in Kyongsong, the house where the Kims stayed to give on-the-spot guidance to the locals is now part of the Kyongsong Revolutionary Museum. There are many more like this all over the country. Local party leaders must live in fear that the Leader will spend the night when he pops by.

Around the corner, behind the bushes, is a vast tiled square with a group of statues of Kim Il-sung surrounded by smiling farmers of conveniently shorter stature.

'We will now pay respect!' our minder announces.

We do what is required. Thankfully, Kim Kubrick is not there to record our bowing for posterity.

'We will now visit the farm!'

We stroll past some fields where farmers in mud-coloured clothes are beavering away. The vivid green of the rows of cabbages stands out against the leaden sky. In the middle a placard bellows a revolutionary slogan. Inside a massive greenhouse courgettes are grown; very large flowers are drooping under the weight of the deluge of water to which they have just been subjected. Our minder drones on about production figures that mean nothing to us. We admire the healthy state of the vegetables but are quickly herded out. The visit is over! We are now led past some rather in-teresting-looking traditional farmhouses and their new modern replacements, which look positively monstrous in comparison. Some groups are allowed a viewing of a carefully selected and doc-tored 'real farm with happy farmers', but we are not. In fact, during our stay, we do not see one single family home from the inside.

North Korea is the only country in the world where all farming is collective. In the 1950s all farmers were expropriated and forced to work in state-run cooperatives. A farmer is allowed only a private plot of 10m^2 maximum. This is very different from the former Soviet Union, where farmers were allowed private plots of up to ten times larger. The 4 per cent of arable land that was farmed privately in the Soviet Union produced one third of the country's total production.

When the famine came, the laws forbidding private farming were ignored by the rural population. They carved out plots to cultivate on tree-covered hills and mountains, as satellite photos have shown. It is estimated that private farming now contributes up to 20 per cent of the food supply of North Korea.

In 2012 Kim Jong-un introduced two significant changes in the law. Production teams on cooperative farms traditionally consisted of fifteen people, but it is now permitted to have teams of five or six. In other words: family farming is back. In addition, whereas originally farmers had to surrender their entire harvest to the state, they are now allowed to keep 30 per cent to themselves. This led to an increase in food production.

We walk towards a three-storey building with a low-fenced playground in front. All is still, until we come near, and then music starts and the fifty-odd toddlers who were waiting in rows start dancing. Three teachers keep an eye on them from the school steps: one plays the accordion, another conducts and a third is on hand to mete out discipline. Accordions were always popular in North Korea as they are easy to carry along on marches, or when the workers need encouraging. The kiddies now start singing and dancing to revolutionary songs. I can clearly discern the hallowed names of Kim Il-sung and Kim Jong-il. They are perhaps five years old (or seven or eight, if they are underfed). They are warmly dressed, with red being the colour of 'choice'. They sing and dance in sync with some enthusiasm: performing must be more fun than sitting inside their unheated classrooms. In the corner of the playground stands the cutest little tank to play in during breaks. After three songs, every child grabs the hand of a long-nosed foreign devil and we join in, holding their tiny, little hands, dancing in a circle, first clockwise, then anti-clockwise. They seem to enjoy themselves, and we do, too.

I wonder how often they have to dance with tourists. Some in our group later say that the way in which the regime forces the children to sing and dance for tourists is tantamount to child abuse.

We arrive at an impressive gate at the foot of Mount Ryonggak. There is a huge billboard with cartoon-like representations of what can be seen en-route to the top of the mountain. Next to the entrance is a lake with a colonnaded walkway, a bridge and two temples, all in the pagoda-picturesque style. It is unclear whether these were built a long time ago, or last week. I suspect concrete below the colourful paint. The buildings are pretty: the red and copper-green of the roofs and the cherry trees blossoming with white flowers contrast beautifully with the milky-white sunless sky. We have been told by Mrs Kim to go to the loo beforehand as there are none at this restaurant; but as we walk the short, steep incline we distinctly see a 'toilets' sign and hurry to it. They are not very clean. When North Koreans say that something isn't there when it patently is, they merely mean to 'protect' the foreigner from something he shouldn't see.

At barely 15 degrees, this must be a hot day for the frost-bitten locals: they've decided that we are going to have an outdoor barbecue. The part of the hill reserved for the outdoor restaurant is covered in concrete slabs with concrete paths in between, all of this embellished with huge life-size dragons in concrete. Concrete mushroom-shaped stools surround the low, concrete tables.

A petite metal-wire barbecue on each table will be used to cook the meal for the eight or so seated around it. Thankfully they use charcoal here. That is a luxury fuel in North Korea: the locals more often than not use petrol for their Sunday roast; they then kill the aftertaste by getting drunk on home-brewed moonshine before they pass out.

'I think that's chicken,' my co-traveller Kate says, pointing at it with a fork. 'Who would like this piece?'

We look at the pale morsel of fat, and nobody responds.

Ladies in traditional hoop-dress come and add 'meat' to the barbecue when we are obviously not doing this properly or not fast enough. Some minute plates of vegetables are also provided. And the ubiquitous beer: one bottle is included with every meal. With the wind blowing from all directions in quick succession, we are all being smoked out. Next to the open-air restaurant are some amusements for children: rides on colourful little tanks and fighter planes; and a little shooting range with plastic Kalashnikovs.

We drive to Pyongsong, 32km northeast of Pyongyang. This mid-sized provincial city (population 285,000) arose from the dusty plain in 1969. We are booked to visit a primary school but it takes a lot of back and forth driving between two blocks before the driver finds it. It's a low, white building with lots of windows. The grim headmistress receives us in her office while the Great Leaders watch us from the wall behind her. Her computer screen is turned towards us so we can see that it's actually CCTV with sharp images of every class.

We pass through the semi-dark corridors. The walls have painted murals of cool teenagers in open-neck red shirts throwing Molotov cocktails. For good measure there is also a poster with missiles, and some black-and-white photos feature babies being bayonetted by the Japanese while crying mothers are made to watch. And then there is a photo of the captured USS *Pueblo*, with the captured American seamen lined up with their hands on their heads. Playing with guns must be positively encouraged in this establishment. One particularly vivid poster catches my eye, and I ask Mr Chong what it says.

'It says: "We will resist the enemy to the last drop of our blood".'

He urges me to follow the others. He is now so used to me not marching in sync that he frowns when I'm in sight. We are led from class to class.

The natural history class consists of two rooms. The anteroom has shelves with badly preserved frogs in cloudy jars of formaldehyde. It takes a while before I identify the blackened creature in the corner as a decomposing seal with its head missing. I avert my eyes. The room next door is large. An imaginative teacher came up with the idea of not having boring educational posters, and has fashioned a colourful three-dimensional plaster display instead. It is quite something, and I can imagine the kiddies' sparkling eyes when they are let into this magical kingdom. In the middle is a large colourful maquette of the entire Korean peninsula, mountains and all. One can switch on lights pinpointing the seven sites of natural beauty and the big cities. Even the birthplace of Kim Il-sung and the two sites to launch missiles are indicated by way of cute little lights. The far wall has a plaster mountain reaching up to the ceiling with all the fauna of Korea: stuffed or imitation life-size sloths, bears, a *papier-mâché* tiger, a unique animal that appears to be a cross between a llama and a giraffe, squirrels, rats etc. All around the room on shelves and on the floor are other stuffed animals covered in a thick layer of dust and in different states of decomposition. There is a maquette to show how animals hibernate underground. Three proud storks look in different directions, one of which is to the floor as its neck suffered fatal trauma a decade or so ago. A large mural painting shows how to find the Great Bear in the night sky. As they are unsure what our reactions to all of this mean, we are quickly shepherded on.

The children in one class rehearsed a song for us; in another one they are working on computers. And in yet another, the kids enthusiastically participate in short English conversations, underlined by studied hand gestures and facial expressions.

Then it's Time for Movement: first we enter a beginners' level ballet class where pre-pre-pubescent girls in pink tutus show us the classical moves. This is followed up by an advanced class for eleven-year-olds. They swirl to electronic modern dance tunes: kiddie pelvises are pushed provocatively in the air, their fabric-shortage glitter dresses covering virtually nothing. They gyrate and churn as if holding onto a pole. These children also wear make-up. We all find this performance disturbing and stop taking photos straight away.

Next we visit the sports hall, which has about twenty ping-pong tables and lots of boys and girls in red shorts and T-shirts ping-ponging fanatically. We are encouraged to push one aside and show off our abilities! The eight-year-old girl against whom I play looks bored and tries to let me win. I haven't ping-ponged for donkey's years but I'm not bad and so I try a few hard balls and backspins. She makes the tiniest little effort and beats me five times.

At the end of our tour of the primary school, we come across arguably the most disturbing sight of our entire stay.

We are shown into another bright and airy classroom with clean, whitewashed walls and very small, yellow chairs. On the walls are collages of black-and-white photos featuring war atrocities, bombing, maimed children and crying mothers.

'Once a week the pupils come in here to learn about their class enemies,' the headmistress drones on, a naughty smile on her face, as if she has just told us a risqué story.

'Class enemies?' I ask, all innocence.

She is not in the least bit embarrassed.

'Yes, the American imperialists and the Japanese war criminals.'

'Ah,' I say.

It saves on re-education afterwards if the correct world view is taught from the word go. It also makes for less-crowded concentration camps. Indoctrination doesn't start in primary school, but in kindergarten. Toddlers receive presents on the Leader's birthday, hear stories about his good deeds, and learn their first songs to praise the Sun of Korea.

In fact, it does not matter what class pupils are in: they will invariably be taught to hail the Great Leader and hate the enemy.

One verse of 'Shoot the Yankee Bastards', a famous song taught to all North Korean schoolchildren goes:

> 'Our enemies are the American bastards,
> who are trying to take over our beautiful fatherland.
> With guns that I make with my own hands
> I will shoot them, BANG, BANG, BANG.'

Originality in thought or problem solving is aggressively put down (though one friend opined that this feature of educational establishments is not limited to North Korea).

Outside in the playground is a noticeboard painted with happy-looking slogans with exclamation marks. I pose for a photo and am told off by American minder Josh: 'For future reference, don't pose for a photo against that background. They will tell you off!'

I look at him, puzzled. Does he really think a photo against a background of slogans is going to cause the demise of the DPRK?

He pulls some knowing frowns, and glances over his shoulder back at me.

I wonder what's wrong with him.

We can't arrive in the new city of Pyongsong without paying our respects to the Great Leaders' statues. I am surprised that this is only our *second* activity since our arrival in this city. The guy in charge of the square, in uniform and with an impressive kepi, rushes towards Mrs Kim and demands to see her ID. He looks suspicious, fearing a 'situation'. Does he think there is something untoward about foreigners paying 'homage' to the interplanetary geniuses who are guiding this country to ever higher levels of world-domination? Down the road, slogans are shouted through a megaphone for no apparent reason. The hotel is nearby, and in the morning we will have learned that the shouting down the megaphone is a 24/7 pursuit.

In the hotel's cavernous reception hall they are saving on the lightbulbs. We are told to shower between eight and ten tonight or between six and eight tomorrow, when there will be hot water. They are not frugal on heating though. The floor heating is on at something like twenty-five degrees and cannot be controlled from the individual rooms, so we all sleep with the doors wide open. The dining hall is about the size of half a football pitch too, with by far the largest oil painting I have ever seen in my life, probably about 20m long. It features a bucolic landscape with mountains, lakes and waterfalls in bright blues, aquamarines and pinks.

CHAPTER NINE

THOSE FROM THE WRONG CLASS STAND IN THE BACK ROW

At six I'm woken by a van with a megaphone strapped on its roof, which tours the carbo-dusted streets while it blares out revolutionary marching music. When I drowsily step out onto the balcony to see what the heck is going on, I shiver. It's pretty cold this morning and I can see my breath. Opposite the hotel I spot about thirty women in green army uniforms holding red flags and dancing in neat rows.

'It's for the 70-Day Campaign,' Mrs Kim tells me later. 'Those are housewives who are not working, so they encourage other people to work.' The British employment programmes are missing a trick.

I note how grim the streets and the surroundings are. Right in front of the hotel, on the cracked car park, lies a pile of rubble. From the left wing of the hotel, the Kims are grinning at me. In this town everything seems a bit greyer; the slogans on the boards shout a bit shriller; and the Kims on every public building are larger and more menacing.

On the bus Mrs Kim marvels about the heat in our bedrooms

last night. North Koreans love being slow-cooked. For them it is a great luxury: apart from a few apartment blocks in Pyongyang that enjoy underfloor heating on the days it functions, there is no such thing as central heating. Temperatures of minus thirty are not uncommon in winter; Pyongyang has an average of thirty-seven days of snow a year. So how do the population heat their houses? Coal and firewood used to be available with rationing coupons, but now they have to be bought. With very few trees remaining and new tree planting being protected, one cannot just get some logs from the woods. Primitive coal-burning stoves in small cramped rooms regularly asphyxiate their users. Some burn the straw remnants of the rice plant. People insulate their houses with all the materials they can find; for example, creating an indoor greenhouse effect by way of plastic sheeting. At the height of the economic crisis and before illegal markets had somewhat jumped into the breach, winter was the time when people froze to death.

It's still very early and the weather is not improving: overcast, drizzly and ice-cold. Our ears nearly freeze off at the Korean Heroes' War Cemetery. It was opened just three years ago by Kim Jong-un to celebrate the sixtieth anniversary of the end of the Korean War. There is the usual large, paved square with gigantic carved soldiers in the heroic workers' style. In the middle is a statue of a huge vertical bayonet.

'King Jong-un himself redesigned the bayonet, so it now has a perfect form,' the minder in long, black velvet robe with diamanté sequins and regulation socialist perm states. She dwells on this for some time, carefully outlining what the bayonet looked like before

Kim took up his magic pencil. We are not quite sure what the point is.

The hill serves as a semi-circular amphitheatre for the small marble tombstones of soldiers. Their corpses were picked especially for reburial here because of the heroic nature of their exploits.

'There are four women, too,' our minder says. 'All of these soldiers are decorated heroes of the fatherland!'

Each tombstone has a black-and-white photo, the name preceded by 'Comrade' in Korean, and the date of their birth and death. Most are boys aged eighteen, nineteen and twenty: lives cut short because Sun Tyrant Kim willed it. The minder tells us some of their stories. One threw a grenade back. Another died trying to carry his wounded friend to safety. The guide skilfully spins the invented Korean War history narrative around these very real deaths.

'How many Chinese died in North Korea?' I ask testily.

'100,000,' she says.

'They are always lying,' Australian Pete whispers in my ear.

It was closer to half a million.

'How many Russians?' my Lithuanian friend asks even more cheekily.

'None,' she says. Her mouth is a horizontal line. Her cheeks are flat with no laughter dimples.

This is actually true. Russia let the Chinese and the North Koreans do the fighting, and sent money and weapons instead.

After a while I am bored and start to wander between the graves, sad and pensive, glancing at the baby-faces of the fallen. Mr Chong follows me quickly, and urges me to go back to the group, grabbing my arm. They must have warned him in spy school about trouble-makers like me.

It's not all sadness. Ironically, the family members of these war-dead have been extremely lucky: they are the highest social class.

For centuries Korea had a feudal class system. The higher class were the happy recipients of never-ending bribes, official positions and privileges. It is still thus: the symmetry between feudal Korea and today's communist Korea is striking.

After Japan won the first Sino-Japanese war and forced China to agree to Korea's independence, it abolished the Korean class system by way of the Kabo Reforms of 1894. The corrupt bureaucracy was professionalised; the king's powers were reduced; advancement based on nepotism was abolished; and slavery and underage mar-riage were banned.

Kim Il-sung re-introduced a hereditary class system known as *song-bun* based on loyalty to his leadership. From 1957 onwards the authori-ties allocated every North Korean into three different classes: the 'loyal' class, the 'complex' class and the 'hostile' class (the 'Inner Party', the 'Outer Party' and the 'Proles' in *Nineteen Eighty-Four*). North Korea's Ministry of Public Security annually issues a 'Resident Registration Project Reference Manual' to explain to government officials how to stratify the people. It contains instructions on whom to enfranchise and whom to disenfranchise. In 1973, Kim Jong-il ordered a three-year country-wide review of all the members of the Workers' Party of Korea to purge older members and replace them with 600,000 young ones loyal to him. Since 2003 the data of each person's *songbun* have been digitised by North Korea's Ministry of Public Security for easier access. This computer data-management system designed to streamline human rights violations is called 'Faithful Servant 2.0'.

The class system is patrilineal: all the male descendants inherit the *songbun* of their parents. It's a bit looser for women: they become part of their husband's family after marriage. Those who are of better *songbun* generally don't like 'marrying beneath them', so the discrimination originated by the state has consequences for private social interaction as well.

The loyal class consists of those who helped the Kims come to power and who maintain the regime: soldiers who fought against the Japanese or in the Korean War (like the ones buried here in this cemetery); civilians who died during the war; discharged soldiers; and those who are deemed to be loyal for other reasons.

The hostile class are former landlords and wealthy people; entrepreneurs; those labelled spies; Buddhists and Catholics; those who worked loyally for the Japanese or the Americans; businessmen who employed workers before 'liberation' (even if they helped Kim Il-sung afterwards); family of defectors to the South; agricultural foremen employed by landowners; merchants; shamans, geishas and fortune tellers. They are deemed disloyal to the leadership. They are treated as being beyond redemption.

The complex class are the in-betweens. They are under suspicion, but can redeem themselves by showing loyalty. It is thought that constant indoctrination is needed to keep them on the straight and narrow. They comprise soldiers who were prisoners of war in the South; draft dodgers; South Koreans who defect to North

Korea; Japanese Koreans who moved back to North Korea in the 1950s and 1960s; and people arrested for alleged ordinary, political or economic crimes.

Apart from being largely hereditary, one's class is subject to 'guilt by association': your *songbun* also depends upon the *songbun* and the deeds of your relatives. It is difficult to improve one's class unless one does something truly brilliant, like saving the Kims' portraits from a burning house. Somebody from the hostile class may rise to become complex class, but it is almost impossible for them to rise to loyal class. A combination of factors may offer a slight improvement of one's *songbun*: e.g. a Pyongyang education or party membership. But those routes are not open to the hostile class. One's class and that of one's family to the third degree can decline, e.g. for a conviction for an ordinary crime. Those convicted of political crimes, e.g. making a joke about the dictatorship, automatically become hostile class. If one person defects to South Korea the entire family's *songbun* nosedives to rock-bottom.

Those from the complex and the hostile class will be discriminated against throughout their lives. They will receive fewer food rations under the Public Distribution System; they cannot attend the best schools; they receive less medical attention; and are given less desirable housing. They will be allocated menial jobs in unpleasant places. Their most typical fate is to be carted off to the inclement industrial zones in the north-east. Because of guilt-by-association in the third degree, it is perfectly possible for a person with high *songbun* who lived in Pyongyang to be expelled to a mine in the north because one of his family members fled to the South. Such 'Pyongyang evacuees' are despised by the low *songbun* people who already live in the unpleasant area to which they are exiled. *Songbun* also plays a role in court sentencing. If one, for example, is being investigated by the security services for a political crime, the records of the entire family play a part in considering whether or not the suspect can be reformed.

Somebody from the hostile class is unlikely to be admitted to membership of the Korean Workers' Party (nobody with a South Korean connection can join any party organisation). North Korea has universal conscription for the Korean People's Army, but those with a physical handicap and those belonging to the hostile class are excluded and cannot serve in it. Not having served in the army is harmful for future career prospects. Within the army, those from a high class can make faster promotion, and get assigned to pleasant and lucrative postings (e.g. a border guard along the Chinese border where one will receive a large amount of bribes from those who want to cross it).

The illegal re-introduction of free market activity has alleviated some of the injustice of the *songbun* system. Those with a bad *songbun* are able to earn money through their own effort and buy their way out of many disadvantages by way of bribes, though it is of course those with good *songbun* who receive the bribes. A bit like the nouveau riche in all societies, those with low *songbun* can even buy their place into the loyal class by way of marriage. The newly rich try to join the loyal class, rather than to rebel against it.

But there is more. One can also buy a better *songbun* by bribing officials or by having one's documentation fabricated.

Notwithstanding all this, 67 per cent of defectors to South Korea in 2014 classified the continuing discrimination in North Korea on the basis of *songbun* as 'severe'.

'Was your family from Pyongyang originally?' I ask Mrs Kim.

'Not originally, no. We came from Hamhung, at the East Sea.'*

'So they were allowed to move to Pyongyang? Why did they move?'

'My father did something, and that is why we moved.'

I ask no further. Only the loyal class and some from the complex class are allowed to live in Pyongyang (the ratio is about 80/20 per cent). Even the happy few who are allowed to live in Pyongyang face discrimination on the basis of having different *songbun*. The 80 per cent will be called upon to stage mass events when, for example, foreign dignitaries visit the city. The 20 per cent will not be called upon (I guess most do not shed tears over that). Only for very grand events will the entire population of Pyongyang be told to attend. But even then, those with lower *songbun* will be placed in less favourable rows in the back.

Frozen stiff from our stay at the cemetery, we are now on our way to visit the Pyongyang Metro. There are only two official metro lines under Pyongyang. Rumour has it that there is a third secret one for military and governmental use only. In 1972 twice as many Chinese metro vehicles were delivered than Pyongyang needed. In 2009 Hwang Jang-yop, the highest-ranking North Korean defector to date (he invented the Juche philosophy and was Chairman of

---

* The East Sea is what North Koreans call the Sea of Japan.

the Standing Committee of the Supreme People's Assembly) told a Seoul radio station that he had visited a secret network of tunnels below the official metro, which links military installations and official buildings, and which offers an escape route in case of disorder. According to Hwang, 'they were so elaborately built that a visiting Soviet military delegation marvelled at them'. After his defection, Hwang's wife 'committed suicide'; his daughter died when she 'fell off a truck'; and his other son and daughter and grandchildren 'disappeared'. Hwang himself was found dead in his bath-tub in 2010.

We are apparently let in for free. For ordinary Pyongyangites, a metro ride costs five won, which, at its devalued rate, is less than one penny (sterling). At some places 150m deep, the *official* Pyongyang metro is the deepest in the world. At the bottom you can see the thick anti-radiation doors: this is, of course, a nuclear shelter. The Great Leaders are watching us, set off against a pink background. We walk down some more marble stairs, until we are at the domed concourse. It's like the Moscow metro: lofty vaulted platforms are lit by colourful crystal chandeliers as if they are drawing rooms. The walls are decorated with mosaics of happy farmers on orange tractors driving over flower-covered roads. Civil engineers with measuring sticks and construction plans are guiding the workers to a brighter future along joyously smoking factory chimneys. An official Pyongyang Metro pamphlet from 1994 stated that the metro's inside decoration 'conveys to posterity the glorious revolutionary history and the leadership exploits of the Great Leader President Kim Il-sung'. There is no graffiti anywhere.

In the middle of the platform is a glass display board where you can read the Workers' Party's newspaper *Rodong Sinmun*. Today's topical news stories include black-and-white photos of Japanese wartime atrocities, as well as the requisite photos of Kim Jong-il. A 2013 report found that North Korea's two main news publications publish more than 300 Kim-related articles a month. All writings are subject to the censorship of the Korean Workers' Party's Propaganda Department. Violating censorship standards may lead to up to ten years in a concentration camp. Reporters Without Borders ranks North Korea 180th out of 180 countries in its 2017 Press Freedom Index report.

On the end wall there is another gorgeous mosaic of factory chimneys emitting pink smoke against a yellow sky. A red electricity pylon completes the 'Triumph of Socialist Industry'. Workers with white teeth in various uniforms are marching towards the socialist paradise. A stout housewife is part of the melee and right in the middle stands the beaming Great Leader. He must have been very tall.

We are at 'Resurrection' station and we will travel five stations away, Mrs Kim explains. We will first do one stop, step out there to look around, and then do four more stops to 'Triumph' station. Each station is named in socialist parlay, e.g. Red Star, Complete Victory, Comrade etc. We are warned to stay together. We need not fear: Mr Chong covers our backs. He feels a bit like a policeman.

We cannot just hop onto the first train screeching into the station. Inexplicably, we seem to be waiting for a very precise one. We are told that when the 'right' train arrives, we will have to enter the first compartment, and no other. So we wait. And wait. About five trains pass before Mrs Kim give the thumbs up and we stream into compartment one.

Inside it's all cosy, dark wood.

'These trains were made in the DPRK,' Mrs Kim says with a straight face.

In fact, these trains are hand-me-downs from the East Berlin Metro. North Korea saved them from the scrapyard in 1996 and 1998 (some earlier trains were bought in China, but the German ones proved more reliable). In trains for showcase visits like ours, all references to Eastern Germany have been carefully removed. Metro enthusiasts point out that traces of the Berliner Verkehrs-betriebe (BVG) emblem can still be discerned between the driver and first passenger doors. One BBC journalist reported in 2000 that there were trains which still had their original German graffiti.

We observe our fellow passengers while the Leaders are watching us. Unlike the other trains we saw pass, this compartment is not busy at all. There are about six passengers and they all sit still and look away, with absolutely no interest in the space aliens who just stepped in. In fact, they look distinctly unnatural. You can just tell: they do not act as normal commuters do. It is utterly bizarre. Are they actors?

We hop out quickly at the Younggwang Station and look around. It is pretty similar to the one we were just at. In the past, tourists were shown only these two stations, leading some to believe that perhaps Pyongyang metro had only two stops.

The entire 80m of the side walls are taken up by a mural of a smiling Kim Il-sung at the helm of a group of smiling workers, engineers and miners. The chimneys emit happy pollutants against a sulphur sky. Hasty commuters pass us by, glancing, but not stopping. We hop onto another train. This time the compartment is full. These travellers are real. They stare at us much in the same way as the Japanese stare: as soon as you look back, they look away, slightly embarrassed for having been so rude as to observe you. They are curious, stealing furtive glimpses of us.

We come out of the depths of the earth again at Arch of Triumph Station.

The Arch is based on the Arc de Triomphe in Paris – but this one is 10m higher. It is rather beautiful, I find, and spectacular. It was built in 1982 on the orders of Kim Il-sung to glorify his alleged role in the military campaign that achieved North Korea's independence from Japan (never mind that independence came about because the Second World War ended). The 25,500 blocks of granite refer to every day of Kim's life up to then. The year 1925 is inscribed: that is when invented Korean history says that Kim set out to fight the Japanese at the improbably tender age of thirteen. It also features the 'General Kim Il-sung Song'. This was composed in 1946 and was the first paean dedicated to Kim Il-sung: the earliest evidence of a personality cult. His son promoted it so heavily from the 1980s onwards that it has now all but replaced the national anthem '*Aegukka*' and is played ahead of it. Percussion and brass instruments are added to give it that extra revolutionary 'oomph'. When North Korea launched its first satellite in 1997, the dictatorship declared that up there it was doing nothing other than continuously playing the Song of General Kim Il-sung, which goes like this:.

Bright traces of blood on the crags of Jangbaek still gleam,
Still the Amnok carries along signs of blood in its stream.
Still do those hallowed traces shine resplendently
Over Korea ever flourishing and free.
So dear to all our hearts is our General's glorious name,
Our own beloved Kim Il-sung of undying fame.

Tell, blizzards that rage in the wild Manchurian plains,
Tell, you nights in forests deep where the silence reigns,
Who is the partisan whose deeds are unsurpassed?
Who is the patriot whose fame shall ever last?
So dear to all our hearts is our General's glorious name,
Our own beloved Kim Il-sung of undying fame.

He severed the chains of the masses, brought them liberty,
The Sun of Korea today, democratic and free.
For the Twenty Points united we stand fast,
Over our fair homeland spring has come at last!
So dear to all our hearts is our General's glorious name,
Our own beloved Kim Il-sung of undying fame.

Lunch is at a restaurant that belongs to the Korean International Travel Company, a state-owned tourist bureau – we are clearly not going to be allowed to eat in any privately run place. Nowadays, substantial businesses are often nominally state-owned, but in reality are private. The private businessmen just bribe the officials: this is why there has been such an increase in the number of restaurants in Pyongyang over the past decade. Jang Sung-taek, the uncle of Kim Jong-un by marriage, was reputed to have amassed private business interests worth $80 million. He fell foul of the regime, though not for his financial affairs. In a 2,700-word statement it was declared that 'the despicable human scum Jang, who was worse than a dog, [had] perpetrated thrice-cursed acts of treachery in betrayal of the profound trust and warmest paternal love shown by the party and the Leader for him.' He was accused of instigating an amnesty in 2012 and closing several concentration camps, building up a private fiefdom that 'nobody dared touch', and disobeying the Leader. In other words: he had become a bit too powerful.

He was executed by machine-gun firing squad.

The food is mediocre, but we do not care: we wolf it up as we are excited about this afternoon's visit. We are going shopping in a real-life North Korean department store.

of restaurants...

CHAPTER TEN

STATE-SPONSORED CRIME

The Kwangbok department store is the only state-owned shop in North Korea where foreigners are allowed to use local currency. Everywhere else we have to use Chinese renminbi, US dollars or euros – at exchange rates that are gloriously extraneous to the international currency rates. The regime makes up currency rates according to how much they like the country. Paying in US dollars is sometimes three times more expensive than paying in Chinese renminbi.

In ordinary shops, prices are advertised in North Korean won, and foreigners have to ask how much that is in renminbi. The shop assistant, seconded by another shop assistant, takes out a big calculator and comes up with an amount that exchanges one Chinese yuan* for, say, 100 won. In this shop, however, one yuan buys ... 1,000 won! So everything is ten times cheaper than elsewhere. When I ask Mr Chong for clarification, he tells me to follow the group. American Josh whispers in my ear that this most propitious

---

* Yuan is the unit of Chinese renminbi.

multiplication of wons has something to do with the devaluation of the currency a few years ago.

North Korea fleeced its population five or six times in this way; the last time was in 2009. The action was aimed at wiping out savings made by 'shameless anti-socialist profiteers in the black market'. Two zeros were chopped off the currency, so 100 won became one won, and theoretically one 'new' won would buy the same as 100 'old' won. The state's hold-up on people's meagre savings was achieved by limiting what one could exchange for new won to 100,000 won (thirty US dollars). At the same time – and this shows the eye-watering economic illiteracy of Kim Jong-il – state salaries were maintained in the old amounts. In other words: salaries went up 100-fold. The people had less than one week to change their old won for new won. Even the Chinese state news agency Xinhua reported panic in the streets. People rushed to the shops to buy all available goods with their old won. Inflation flared up. The death penalty was introduced for private foreign currency exchanges (introducing the death penalty is the regime's default position for any trouble). The rattled government increased the exchange limits to 150,000 won in cash and 300,000 won in bank deposits. It then tried to introduce maximum prices for consumer goods. Like everywhere else at all times when price controls are introduced, the sellers refused to sell for such low prices. Hoarding and shortages ensued. Then the government closed down the 'illegal' markets, as well as the shops where the rich can buy goods with foreign currency. They then made a U-turn and commanded their officials not to interfere in the black markets.

The North Korean Prime Minister was purged; and Pak Nam-gi, a high-ranking official responsible for economic policy, was executed for espionage. By 2010 the prices had stabilised at the same level as before the currency reform.

Since this experience, many North Koreans use Chinese renminbi for business and savings instead of won. Unlike previously in other communist countries, North Koreans never try to exchange won for renminbi with foreigners illegally, as foreigners are not allowed to use the local currency. Foreigners are punished if they possess won when leaving North Korea.

Yet here in the Kwangbok department store foreigners can change their currency into won at a little booth in the back of the supermarket. Why do the authorities allow this?

The re-opening of the Kwangbok department store in 2012 was crowded by high-ups of the Korea Taeson General Trading Corporation. This company is expressly named on the international sanctions lists against North Korea. The US Treasury says that it is a key player in the illicit activities of the nebulous Room 39.

Room 39 is sometimes called Section 39 or Department 39. In North Korea, government departments are often given a number to keep their activities under wraps: Room 35 is the international espionage department; Room 38 is in charge of the Leader's personal wealth; Room 101 is in charge of writing eulogies to the Leader under assumed South Korean names to make North Koreans believe that intellectuals in the South support the Kims. Room 813 produces books purporting to have been printed by South Korean publishers.

Room 39 was set up by Kim Jong-il in 1974 to obtain foreign currency for the Kim family. They need hard currency to buy luxuries for themselves and political support, and to fund the nuclear weapons programme. More than 120 foreign corporations are said to fall under its aegis and it is estimated to bring in about $1 billion a year. It is involved in the industrial-scale counterfeiting of American $100 bills; in producing and selling drugs; in the sale of gold mined in North Korea; in international fraud; and in running the Kwangbok department store we are visiting today. Room 39's commercial activities overlap with espionage and crime. For example, Room 39 runs a large number of North Korean restaurants throughout Asia. Even though the profits from these are relatively minor, the restaurants are also used as money-laundering facilities, for espionage and for blackmail. The restaurants especially like serving too much alcohol to South Korean businessmen, for whom private rooms with microphones and cameras are provided.

Room 39's involvement with drugs is legendary. They didn't invent the practice: both the Japanese and the German governments drugged their soldiers with methamphetamine to give them a feeling of invincibility during the Second World War. State-owned North Korean factories used to produce meth on an industrial scale and it was sold to the Chinese and Japanese market. The production was reduced when China complained, but the activity has now been taken over by private enterprise.

In 2013, the United States redesigned its $100 bill to face off fakes produced in North Korea. The fakes were so perfect that they were dubbed 'supernotes'. A number of North Korean traffickers have been arrested worldwide. The dollars were exported by way of diplomatic post, which under the 1961 Vienna Convention cannot be searched or seized. It is not known whether North Korea also produces other currencies; I am always deeply suspicious when I receive a brand new dollar or euro note in change in North Korea.

The visit to the Kwangbok department store is fascinating. Bear in mind that we have not been given access to any other state-owned shop that is also frequented by North Koreans; up to now we were always completely alone when we visited a shop. The Kwangbok is well-attended, but for some reason the locals look hostile. Maybe they think there will be nothing left to buy after the long-nosed foreign devils have plundered it? In fact, this su-permarket's operational model is revolutionary for North Korea. It has been around for a long time, but it was refurbished and re-opened in 2012. Previously it used to operate as in other commu-nist countries: you had to queue three times before you could take your purchases home. There was one queue to order; another one to pay; and a final one for the pick-up. The Kwangbok has now adopted a Western-style check-out – the first one in North Korea.

The ground floor houses the food section, the electrical appli-ances section and a restaurant. The first floor has mainly clothes. The third floor sells furniture and boasts a second restaurant. As I want to buy a cheap travel bag to bring all the goodies back that I have hoarded over the past days, I don't spend much time in the food section. It does sell what looks like live sturgeons in dirty fish-tanks. There are also ice-boxes containing transparent bags with unidentified meat and fish. The North Korean alcohol looks enticing and it is available in large and varied quantity, but I have no intention of buying any more leaking bottles.

The North Korean-made merchandise is incredibly cheap. But the Kwangbok also sells foreign goods that cost about the same as they do in London. A Siemens washing machine selling for £600 must be completely out of reach for 99.9 per cent of North Koreans. Has it been put here for show? The bicycles look impressive and are one tenth of the London price but I can hardly fold them up in my allocated hand luggage. Up the escalators we go. The clothes are mind-bogglingly cheap: a T-shirt is fifty pence. Sadly the style is rather 'local'. Shoes are cheap, unless they are leather, in which case they cost as much as they do on Oxford Street. One does wonder how locals can afford to spend 7 per cent of their average annual income on a pair of shoes.

Back on the ground floor I am desperate for an ice cream, which Mrs Kim recommended we try. I have some difficulty figuring out how to order it from the ice cream stall; in the end Mrs Kim does the talking and pays for it. I am hugely grateful, because it is delicious and I have been deprived of ice cream for an entire week. It costs her the grand total of ten pence. I don't feel too guilty for eating her meagre income as (a) as a foreigners' minder she must make an absolute fortune in tips, and (2) I did give her a bottle of whisky as a present last week. The travel agency had suggested we do this. For North Koreans, as little as a bottle could constitute the difference between sending their offspring to a good school rather than a poor one. Bottles of alcohol and cartons of cigarettes often function instead of money in a country where the already worthless won constantly devalues more. Poor Mr Chong had to make do with a bar of chocolate, since I brought only one bottle to North Korea.

Because everything is so cheap and unattractive, few in the group have spent the five euros that Mrs Kim had suggested we change into wons. We now all struggle with the momentous decision of whether to keep our quasi-extraterrestrial wons and risk being arrested at the border; or to change them back into euros.

Salaries have little meaning in North Korea as the Leader's munificence theoretically provides for everything from cradle to grave. Until the crisis of the 1990s, all food essentials were rationed by way of the Public Distribution System (non-essential goods were not available). The system was very similar to the Ministry of Plenty in *Nineteen Eighty-Four* which kept the population dependent by providing them with just enough goods, and poor (a wealthy population being more difficult to handle). As such, the Ministry of Plenty was a misnomer, as, instead of providing plenty, it oversaw rationing and shortages. And so it was with North Korea's PDS: your work unit would allocate you coupons for, say, 700g of grain a day; a certain amount of soy sauce and an apple. Housewives or those not carrying out manual labour obtained less. When it was the Leader's birthday, or for any number of other holidays or anniversaries, you would perhaps receive a new suit and the children some toys or new school uniforms. Healthcare and education were free (though good healthcare was and is largely unavailable). Housing was allocated by the state too, and no rent was payable. In other words: your salary was just pocket money. Salaries were mainly saved, as there were no consumer goods for sale. The only things one could spend on liberally were services, e.g. haircuts. To make substantial purchases, e.g. a watch, you needed permission from your work unit. Kim Il-sung boasted that North Korea was the only country in the world where there was no need for money, as each received 'according to need'.

When the economic crisis and the famine struck, the rationing system collapsed. Only the elites still received sufficient rations to survive. State salaries, paid for in worthless won, were insufficient to pay for the additional food needed. This caused the most dramatic change since the communist takeover: after fifty years of being kept like birds in cages, people rediscovered trade and self-help.

All over the country people started to set up market stalls. They were like weeds: if the government shut down a stall or a market, they opened elsewhere.

This parallel economy was often run by housewives, as husbands were still supposed to turn up at their non-operating factories. They increasingly stayed away from their state jobs in order to trade in the market, sometimes for months on end, e.g. if they wanted to smuggle goods from China. It sufficed to bribe their equally hungry superiors to turn a blind eye. Occasionally workers would strip their factories of all that was sellable – at great risk, as this is considered a political offence in North Korea, for which one can be sent to a concentration camp. Even government officials used trade to supplement their income. Sometimes friends or family clubbed together to buy goods to sell in the market, effectively creating share companies. Strictly speaking, capitalist trade and production were illegal, but as most were hungry, few officials enforced the law, and many were susceptible to bribes. Graffiti on the walls asked: 'How otherwise are we supposed to survive?'

Those who stuck to the state rules died from hunger.

Today the state income is usually only a fraction of a family's total income, as most of it derives from trade. This has led to emancipation as women traders now often earn many times more than their husbands. Small private companies exist everywhere. There is now a class of newly rich who spend on consumer goods imported from China; on houses (paid-and-bribed for); and even occasionally on such an outrageous luxury as a private car.

Half an hour later we are in Mangyongdae, a green park-like landscape with trees and shrubs and manicured lawns. It does not look natural, but it is very pleasant indeed. The area is surrounded by several hills, the highest of which is called Mangyong Hill ('Ten Thousand Views Hill'). Up to now we have seen no other parkland; usually every square centimetre of flatland is cultivated with edibles.

Mangyongdae was the place where Kim Jong-il's family allegedly lived, and where he was born. Mrs Kim explains that the Kims were 'very humble farmers'. This must be another lie, as it is hard to believe that these idyllic hills with their sweeping views of Pyongyang were ever anything else than desirable and therefore expensive land.

The Kim family history is murky as most official information has been masticated and refabricated by the regime for more than sixty years. It is illegal to mention any information about the Kim family that does not concord with the official invented history. In the late 1990s, Kim Jong-il ordered that an 'Annals of the Kim Dynasty' be compiled with an annual record of its great deeds; just as had been done during the monarchical Chosun period (1392–1893) by way of the 'Annals of the Chosun Dynasty'. A team of researchers was appointed for this purpose by the United Front Department (this is the department for disinformation). They had direct access to all documents relating to the Kim family, and were tasked with compiling an 'ideologically correct' panegyric based on this. The writers found this to be a rather taxing job as they came across numerous instances where the invented history diverged from the historical documents.

Kim Sŏng-ju was born in 1912, two years after the Japanese occupied Korea. Traditionally, Koreans had seen the Japanese as 'rustics' – so the invasion must have come as a double shock. Kim was the eldest of three sons; the youngest died early and the middle one joined Kim Il-sung in the leadership. He fell out of favour in 1974, and henceforth held the ceremonial position of Vice-President of the North Korean Parliament. Kim's parents were both Christians; indeed, his maternal grandfather had been a Presbyterian missionary. Both Kim's father and Kim played the church organ, something that invented North Korean history never mentions. Originally a farmer, his father became a doctor, treating his patients with traditional medicine. By North Korean standards they were middle class. When he was seven years old his

parents moved from Japanese-occupied Korea to Chinese Manchuria, possibly to escape famine. Kim's Korean started to suffer,
so at the age of eleven he was sent back to his grandparents in
Pyongyang. At the age of thirteen he left again to join his parents
in Manchuria (not to join the Korean guerrillas to fight the Japanese as the invented history tells us). His father died and Jong-il
continued to study, picking up some Marxism from a teacher. His
Soviet teachers later said that he wasn't very good at it. In 1929
Kim was thrown in prison for several months by the Chinese
police for his Marxist activities. The 'Mukden Incident' in 1931
gave the Japanese army an excuse to invade Chinese Manchuria,
even though the Japanese civilian government had not sanctioned
the move. A pro-Japanese government was installed in 1932 with
Puyi, the deposed last Chinese Qing emperor, as puppet emperor
of Manchukuo. As we have seen previously, Kim now joined the
anti-Japanese guerrillas in Manchuria. Some claim that he stole
the name of a famous guerrilla fighter called Kim Il-sung, who had
died. The extent of his guerrilla activities there is unclear: invented
history talks about 'Kim heading the Korean People's Liberation
Army', whereas others say that they were just a handful of Chinese
and Korean students supported by the Soviet Union.

Invented North Korean history alleges that Kim set up a guerrilla camp on Paektu Mountain where his son Kim Jong-il was born.
There is ample evidence that in reality Kim had fled to the Soviet
Union by then. In everyday North Korean panegyrics, the Kim
dynasty is sometimes said to be 'of the Paektu bloodline'. There
is a miraculously well-preserved log cabin on Paektu Mountain

that allegedly housed the Kim family, and which is the official Shrine Number One of the Kim Cult. Just like Christ's barn in Bethlehem, the cabin on Paektu Mountain is often represented in a snowy landscape with a warm glow beaming out of the windows. Aspirational North Koreans love 'paying their respects' at the site. One is taken up in a train of great antiquity – though often the train doesn't work, so one has to make do in the back of an open lorry. Along the way, one mountain flank is defiled by a large inscription hailing Kim Il-sung.*

Up high, the pilgrims can view inside the cabin through the open windows. It is a spartan room with straw mats on the floor and three photos on the wall: that of a middle-aged Kim Il-sung; a photo of Kim Jong-il as a young boy (after all, he was miraculously born here); and of his mother, Kim Sŏng-ju. North Korean pilgrims have their photos taken in the spots where Kim sat, stood and observed the landscape while having gravity-shattering thoughts.

When we dismount from the bus we are told that it will be OK to take photos of Shrine Number Two. We are kept at a slow ceremonial pace, and a winding stone path forces a detour across the well-tended lawn to prolong the approach. Two gardeners on their haunches are engaged in the business of cutting the lawn with scissors. They put the blades of grass in a special basket. This is how full employment is achieved. Out of the trees comes muted stately music.

And there is the alleged birthplace of Kim Il-sung! The

---

* His grandson has done even better: next to a lake in Ryanggang Province he had the message 'Long Live General Kim Jong-un, the Shining Sun!' carved into a hill in letters so large that they can allegedly be seen from space.

landscape around is so beautiful that I immediately suspect that some Kim supporters probably have villas in the vicinity. A few lavish abodes would be so easy to hide among the trees in this high-security zone.

'Oh no,' Mrs Kim states. 'Nobody lives here.'

'But what are those two houses over there then?'

She looks annoyed. 'Those are not houses. They are storage for cleaning materials.'

They are definitely houses.

'But were there no other houses when the Kims lived here? I read somewhere that Mangyongdae was a village?'

'Yes, there were houses, but they were carpet bombed by the American imperialists.'

Such a happy coincidence that of all the houses bombed out, the only one that survived happened to be the Kims'. Perhaps there is something celestial going on after all.

Two very large wreaths on easels stand next to the gate of the house. Our minder, in a long, black velvet robe with diamanté sequins and regulation socialist perm, welcomes us. She beckons us in and guides us from room to room. It's a U-shaped complex of low buildings with thatched roofs, which are open on the courtyard side. Everything looks brand new.

'It's all make-believe, you know,' Australian Pete whispers.

There is a barn on the left; a second barn divided into three rooms on the right; and a third small straw barn at the end that was used for sleeping in summer. With hushed reverence our minder explains how the Kims' parents and grandparents lived here.

'Even the grandfather was already a great revolutionary. He led a peasants' revolt against American imperialists in 1866.'

When General Sherman sailed up the Taedong River, there was indeed an attack by farmers, who set the ship on fire. Grandfather Kim's involvement is tenuous, to put it mildly.

Our guide pays particular attention to the barn on the left, which houses a hard-hitting arsenal of farming tools.

'Can you see that this is a broken jar? It was used to store rice. The family was so poor that they were unable to buy a proper jar,' the guide marvels. For a few seconds she looks into the middle distance, as if in a trance.

On the right is a simple kitchen and two living rooms that served as sleeping quarters at night. There are a few chests and a Western clock on the wall and some black-and-white photos of the family.

'Our Great Leader Kim Il-sung's father was a poor farmer who resisted the Japanese war criminals until he had to flee to Japanese-occupied Manchuria,' she continues.

In reality he was a self-taught middle-class doctor and occasional teacher, who fled the famine.

'He died in Manchuria while continuing to resist the Japanese,' she swoons.

There is absolutely no evidence of this.

'The Great Leader's uncle Kim Hyong-gwon also resisted the Japanese. He attacked a Japanese police station and died in prison in Seoul.'

This family member may, or may not have been, the genuine article. This uncle is an important player in the personality cult of the Kim family. There are several statues of him, and the province of Pungsan was renamed Kim Hyong-won County after him.

'The Leader's brother also died fighting the Japanese.'

She points at his hazy portrait on the wall.

'When, at the age of thirteen, our Great Leader heard that his father had been arrested in Manchuria by the Japanese, he left his family and walked to China to fight the Japanese and only saw this house and his family again twenty years later!'

Our minder's reverence has reached such dizzying heights that I expect her to burst into tears any moment now.

'This is a photo of Kim Il-sung visiting his family when he was already president!'

That the Great Leader should visit his family even when he had to carry the presidential burden is evidence of his divinity.

'The Great Leader's parents continued to live in this simple farmhouse even after Kim Il-sung became president!'

We are shepherded out. Along the path the next pilgrims are already approaching with bouquets of flowers. An entire province must be blanketed with hothouses to grow the flowers for Kim statues and shrines. These are middle-aged men and women dressed in brown, black and dark grey. I wonder how often their work unit has dragged them to this shrine over the years.

The most talented children in Pyongyang with the right *songbun* can go to the Mangyongdae Children's Palace for extra-curricular activities such as sports, learning languages, or music. It is a gigantic rectangular building with two ninety-degree circular side wings.

'Like the arms of a mother,' coos Mrs Kim.

Huge halls in gleaming tiles have been given a whimsical edge by way of pastel-coloured chandeliers. Lots of light streams in through large windows. Like most places in North Korea, the halls are spotless.

We are guided around by a seventeen-year-old girl. She wears a blue pleated skirt and a white blouse with a red scarf tied around her neck. Making robotic movements, she reels off slogans learned by heart. 'Welcome to the Mangyongdae Children's Palace!' she shouts. 'The Mangyongdae Children's Palace was opened by the Great Leader Kim Il-sung on 2 May 1989! It is always full of children who want to follow the example of the Great Leader to build a socialist unified Korea under the guidance of the Juche principles and the Workers' Party of Korea!'

'But it is nearly empty. Where is everybody?' I ask, my eyes searching for people in the cavernous halls.

'They are all preparing for Kim Il-sung's birthday tomorrow!' she says, eyes blazing proudly.

In one of the classes some girls do a dance routine. In another class girls play the traditional *kayagum*, a long wooden stringed instrument with twelve strings. One side rests on the ground, and the other on the girls' laps. They all bear studied smiles, like the smiles of the girls at the school yesterday. We see a calligraphy class (girls). Basketball is played in an enormous sports hall (boys). On the wall is a very large photo of Kim III giving on-the-spot guidance about the rules of volleyball. Four of the six people around him are assiduously recording his wise words. Some lacklustre swimming takes place in a very large designer swimming pool (boys).

Then we take our places in a 2,000-seat theatre. I wonder what we will see here. A play, perhaps? A friend from another group told me yesterday that they were taken to a children's play in the Kim Il-sung Stadium. The play was about American soldiers in the Korean War. It showed the Americans harassing a Korean family. Thankfully their young teenage son managed to kill the 'arrogant Americans'.

There are many more Westerners in the audience than we have seen at any one point in North Korea, even more than during the marathon. It takes a while for the theatre to fill. The North Korean parents of performing children are carefully separated in different rows from us Westerners.

What follows is an hour-long panto of modern music, dancing, singing and theatre.

A girl walks onto the stage and makes a short speech. It's the usual 'hushed emotional reverence' tone; and I can understand nothing except the repeated mentioning of 'Kim Il-sung'. Applause erupts when an image of Kim's nativity house is projected on the screen at the back of the stage. The show is first-rate. Dancing acts with up to 100 performers are interspersed with singing and music. All the little performers have the same uniform of blue trousers or skirts, white shirts and a red handkerchief tied around their necks. The nature scenes projected onto the screen change regularly. Every third or fourth image features one of the Kims, and the audience clap rapturously. Some Westerners who have temporarily taken leave of their senses feel the need to join in the applause. At one point a group of ten-year-old boys perform a strident marching song while the screen shows cartoon images of tanks, gunboats, missiles and military planes. Then Kim comes up again, and the public goes ballistic. Some attempt a standing ovation. Next a screaming slogan on a red background with an exclamation mark makes its inevitable appearance and prolonged applause erupts again. It's probably best that we can't understand the Korean lyrics. All of these marching uniformed little soldiers make me think of the connivances of Jiang Qing, the infamous 'Madame Mao' (Mao's last wife), who replaced China's traditional theatre and music with revolutionary Maoist work. I wonder what traditional Korean music is like. We shall certainly not hear it in this cultural venue.

At the end of the show, some Westerners bring flowers to the stage. Has mad cow's disease turned their brains into mush? No doubt they are being filmed. The guide-robot takes her leave, and we depart for the next stop of our tour: the shooting range.

I guess the shooting range is an attempt by the regime to train its population to shoot American imperialists when they finally opt for a suicidal invasion of the South. The pacifists in our group opt for the bow and arrow option. I go straight for the pistols. It's a hefty one dollar per bullet to shoot the Russian pistol, and fifty cents for the North Korean one. Apart from the price, it's like any other shooting range. Sadly we do not receive our target sheet. Probably best, as my hands shake and I do badly.

We drive to yet another soulless restaurant that serves lots of kimchi and one bottle of beer per person. By now everybody is sleepy; it cannot be said that the programme is for slackers. On the bus home most eyes are closed, and few hear Mrs Kim's announcement that tomorrow will be the highlight of our tour.

CHAPTER ELEVEN

RED-EYED, MEDAL-ENCRUSTED GENERALS

Thanks to the North Korean calendar next to my bed I know that today is an important national day:

April 15, Juche 1 (1912), Day of the Sun. The great leader Comrade Kim Il-sung was born.

I immediately sit up straight, because today we will visit the Sun Tyrant's palace! When Kim Sŏng-ju joined the anti-Japanese guerrillas in 1935 he took on the nom de guerre Kim Il-sung. In English, his adopted name means 'Kim the Sun'. In North Korea, sunrise symbolises Kim's coming to power. The palace where the Sun Tyrant worked used to be known as the Kumsusan Assembly Hall but was renamed 'The Kumsusan Palace of the Sun' in 2012 after it had become his mausoleum. Throughout the week we have been told that the visit of the Palace will be the highlight of our visit.

In death, Kim Il-sung has entered the hallowed realms of

mysticism: because according to the North Korean 'Ministry of Truth', he is alive and kicking! Let me explain.

In 1998, the North Korean Constitution was amended to state that Kim Il-sung is North Korea's 'Eternal President'. This is one step beyond the 'President for Life' title that assorted ragtag African dictators used to award themselves in the second part of the twentieth century. There will never be another President of North Korea again, because Kim the first is still in the driving seat. That's right: the reigning president of North Korea is a corpse.

But then who does the day-to-day running of the country? Who decides who gets the cognac? The corpse governs through its agents. When the Sun Tyrant died, the functions of President were split into three posts: the Prime Minister (head of government); the Chairman of Parliament (head of the legislature); and the Supreme Commander of the National Defence Commission (head of the army). Both Kim Il-sung's son Kim Jong-il, and his grandson Kim Jong-un became head of the army and head of the Workers' Party of Korea. Both were known as 'Supreme Leader', with absolute control over the country.

Later it was decided that his son Kim Jong-il should be the eternal-something too. So he was promoted to Eternal General Secretary of the Workers' Party of Korea and Eternal Chairman of the National Defence Commission of the DPRK. Poor Kim Jong-un therefore has to make do with the title of First Secretary of the Workers' Party of Korea and First Chairman of the National Defence Commission. No doubt he will be elevated to eternity, too. Because of this weird invention of the presidency being bestowed on a corpse, the North Koreans don't say that they are 'going to the mausoleum of Kim Il-sung'.

'We say that we are going to visit Kim Il-sung,' Mrs Kim proudly states.

Those with diverging views automatically qualify for a single to the concentration camp.

The protocol for the mausoleum is the most draconian we've had to follow up to now; it's even stricter than when we visited the Kims' statues. Yesterday we have been told to put our best clothes on. No T-shirts; no sport shoes; no mini-skirts; no sunglasses. Early this morning Mrs Kim is available for pre-emptive sartorial inspection and guidance in the reception hall. For men, a tie is compulsory; some have had to buy one in the smelly hotel shop yesterday. As I could not fit a formal jacket in my roll-on luggage, I have just my leather jacket. Mrs Kim takes one leaden-eyed look.

'It is maybe better if you take it off.'

A white shirt with a tie is apparently more proper than a white shirt with a tie and a leather jacket. I sheepishly do as I'm told.

It does not stop there. We are not to laugh or joke. In fact, we are not to talk at all. We are not to cross our arms, or have our hands in our pockets: we should hold our arms and hands on the side of our bodies. Mrs Kim demonstrates this.

So there we all are: à la mode de Pyongyang, with ties brought, bought or borrowed; measuring each other up. Mrs Kim is in her wedding dress: her *hanbok* national hoop-attire is bluer than the sky.

At the VIP parking of the mausoleum we are shepherded into

an ante hall, a bright and airy reception villa where we can go to the loo for the last time, or brush up or whatever. It's not entirely clear why we have to wait here. Is this to build up momentum? Or have we booked a slot, and did we arrive early? You wouldn't want to arrive late to meet the Great Leader.

Several cars with blackened windows and diplomatic number plates halt in the parking lot. Suited and uniformed grandees step out and jump the queue ahead of us. When it is finally our turn, we are given last instructions by Mrs Kim. Then we walk into a long corridor, in a slow dignified manner. At the cloakroom we have to check in our cameras and are told not to wear electronic watches and to switch our phones off. Leaving some money in our pockets is OK, but nothing else.

'Mrs Kim, I would like to keep some tissue-paper in my pocket. My nose is running like a tap.'

She hesitates.

'That's OK,' she grudgingly nods, looking doubtful.

Our shoes are 'cleansed' by way of a brushing machine. Then follows a 400m travellator. Smiles are banned. Specially composed solemn music hums from a celestial distance. On the white walls left and right of the travellator are large snaps of the Leaders in elaborate gold frames. Benign smiling Kims; giving on-the-spot guidance Kims; Kims-in-the-snow; Kims-meeting-other-tyrants; two Kims; three Kims. I try not to appear too interested in order not to give any credence to the regime. The travellator on the other side is returning red-eyed North Korean soldiers to the exit. The travellator' pace is slow so as to prolong the approach; and Mrs Kim does not walk on them but just stands sill, and we behind her.

We then have to pass through a security arch, and a stern-looking decorated major demands I empty my pocket. His white-gloved hands inspect the wet tissue I just blew my nose into.

We are finally in the mausoleum proper. The size of the palace is difficult to describe. Halls of tens of metres long by tens of metres wide and ten metres high are the norm. All is marble. Crystal dangles from faraway ceilings. The polished mahogany double-doors between rooms are vast and lined with abundant gold detailing. Lots of palace clerks and stiff soldiers look stern and officious.

This, the official residence of Kim Il-sung, was built in 1976: well before the economy collapsed, the GDP halved and the people started dying in the streets. In fact, one could say Kim Il-sung died at a convenient time: his policies created the crisis but he was never blamed for it as disaster struck just after his death. I do wonder whether during his lifetime people knew he was living and working there; or whether it was a state secret just like Kim III's abode is today.

After his father's death in 1994 and during the famine, Kim Jong-il turned the palace into his father's mausoleum at a trifling $900 million. The layout was changed, the windows were bricked up, and an elaborate air-conditioning system was installed to keep the temperature a cool constant.

We enter a hall with a life-like oil portrait of Kim I and Kim II with a kitschy Paektu Mountain in the background. We have to stop at a yellow line and an unsmiling white-gloved major-domo inspects us one by one to see whether we are properly dressed.

Notwithstanding the grave responsibilities of his offices, and with frowning of the utmost severity, he finally lets us through. We go up in a marble-lined lift and walk through a space-age machine that is supposed to blow the dust from our clothes. We have to walk in single file. We tell each other off for not doing it properly: just like good North Koreans we are self-policing and crawling for the regime already.

A crumpled general takes priority. His medals are plastered from his collar to the bottom seam of his jacket. He is supported by a walking stick and two strappy youths.

We know we are about to enter the mummy-room because a reddish glow escapes from the huge open doors in the distance.

A slow funeral step and stately music lead us in. We are to walk in rows of four, carefully choreographed and overseen by many expressionless soldiers. The room is a cube of about 30m. The walls are covered in red granite. Dimmed light morphs everything in a red other-worldly glow. It is not something one can easily forget. The heavy glass coffin stands on a podium in the middle.

And there is the mummy! At a distance of about 8 or 10m, lying on its back, face looking upwards. It has been doctored. During his lifetime Kim Il-sung developed a goitre behind his right ear the size of a tennis ball. All photographs were always taken from his left side, so the North Koreans never saw the physical imperfection of the Sun Tyrant. If photos showed the growth they were deleted by the censors (what happened to the photographers is not recorded). Even though a goitre is caused by an enlargement of the thyroid gland and removal is relatively safe, North Korean doctors were too scared to remove it, and Kim Il-sung was too scared of doctors.

The mummy is wax-like and unreal. There is of course a con-spiracy theory doing the rounds that it is a fake; just as with the bodies of other famous communist dictators that were turned into mummies. Kim Il-sung has joined a select club of mass-murderers consisting of Lenin, Mao, Ho Chi Minh, Stalin and Klement Got-twald. Some eccentric travellers make it their quest to visit all the sites in the world.

In the case of Lenin, the communist regime had wanted to go one step further by preserving the body cryogenically, in order to revive him in the future. The equipment was purchased abroad, but the plan was abandoned. The Russian government paid for the preservation of Lenin's mummy until 1991. Since then the preser-vation has ironically been continued thanks to private donations. He can't turn in his grave.

Stalin's mummy was displayed next to Lenin's in the mausoleum in Red Square in Moscow; but later Khrushchev ordered its re-moval. Stalin was then buried next to other leaders of the Russian Revolution near the Kremlin wall.

Klement Gottwald, the first communist president of Czecho-slovakia, was displayed in a mausoleum in Prague. By 1962 the personality cult was over and his body had started decomposing because of shambolic embalming. The putrefied remains were cremated, and now lie buried with twenty other communists in a common grave.

Just three years ago, an attempt was made to mummify the body of President Hugo Chavez, the man who destroyed Venezuela's prosperity. The world's leading embalmers were flown in from

Russia and Germany. 'Unfortunately' the body was already too far decomposed to have it mummified.

How is it done? It is like pickling food: you create a sterile environment. The chemical composition of the tissues are changed and the bacteria are gotten rid of so no fungus can grow. The blood is taken out, and the body is treated with glycerol, alcohol and formalin. The process is regularly repeated. Pink dye is added to the formalin to give the body a life-like look. A wig is provided because the chemicals make the hair fall out. The climate is carefully controlled. Eventually the chemicals start to leak through the clothes, so these have to be replaced regularly.

Via an elaborate cordoned-off track we approach the mummy. We step forward, four at a time, guided by a master of ceremonies. We bow at the mummy's feet; walk around to the left and bow at its right side (starboard); then walk around the head-side and bow again at its left side (port-side). It has to be a full bow from the waist; not a simple head bow. Then we are shepherded out.

Kim Il-sung's death in 1994 was kept from the public for two days after it occurred. The funeral committee, headed by his son Kim Jong-il, declared an official mourning period of ten days, during which no amusements such as drinking alcohol were allowed. On top of that came an 'ordinary' mourning period of three years, during which Kim Jong-il 'did not take up full leadership of the country out of respect'. Those who violated the mourning period were punished. In 2014, the twentieth anniversary of Kim Il-sung's death, another ten-day mourning period was announced. As he is called 'the Eternal President', the anniversaries of his death are called 'Celebrations of Kim Il-sung's Eternal Life'.

The funeral committee decided that foreign mourning delegations would not be received. Since relationships with the West were strained and most of the former communist countries had turned capitalist, North Korea was already firmly isolated. They avoided the indignity of nobody turning up.

The film of Kim Il-sung's funeral on YouTube is a sight to behold. It's full of images of hysterical North Koreans crying, beating their fists against tree trunks, running to the statues to pay homage. The hearse leaving the Kumsusan Palace (still with real windows; it's not yet turned into a tomb) looks suspiciously like an American stretch-limo. One lone soldier is goose-stepping next to it. A shockingly lean red-eyed Kim Jong-il and assorted red-eyed generals watch the car pass by. Soldiers carry silver AK47s and military bands play heroic marches. The voiceover is done by a presenter with awed and quivering voice. The whole population has been told to turn up. They stand watching the funeral procession, twenty deep. Perhaps those with feeble nerves have been put in the front row because many are crying. Or were they ordered to do so? Interestingly, even the images the cameramen choose to record for live broadcast show people in the background who are *not* crying, and looking quite stoical. It is known that at mass events where the entire population of Pyongyang is ordered to attend, those with higher *songbun* are given front rows, and the 'lesser beings' are forced to stand in the back. Half the army, including tank columns, follow the hearse. There is also a car with a huge portrait of Kim Il-sung mounted on top. Kim Jong-il has ordered that henceforward portraits and statues of his father should be smiling, 'as he is alive forever'.

In the next scenes the Kim-mummy lies in a glass box. One wonders: he cannot have been *in* his coffin on the hearse when it was carried through Pyongyang; the cortege took place a full eleven days after he died. He must already have been embalmed in his air-conditioned glass box. What the mourners saw must have been an empty coffin. In a country where most of history has been made up by the regime, this is small fry.

Western diplomats are shown signing the book of condolences. Throughout the night, endless crowds pass by the illuminated mummy. Crying Young Pioneers make a bizarre half-Nazi-like salute (flat hand held at forty-five degrees upwards in front of their face). Thousands kneel at the statues; the kow-towing as for yesteryear's Chinese emperors is alive and well in North Korea. Huge funeral wreaths are brought to Kim statues and memorials all over the country.

Hysterical scenes at the funerals of North Korean leaders are almost incomprehensible to Westerners. Attendance at the spectacles was compulsory. Attendance at the statues was too, and this was encouraged through the distribution of gifts. Hysteria is infectious, of course. You couldn't get away with *not* mourning the departing of the Leaders. One wonders which tricks the attendees used in order to obtain teary eyes. For many, the grief may have been genuine: being told for seventy-five years that you could not go on without the Leader, with no outside information telling you otherwise, would have a marked effect on many.

In another cavernous marble hall stands Kim Il-sung's personal armoured train wagon. The Great Leader was afraid of flying. When I ask Mrs Kim how they got the wagon in the palace's room, she can't answer.

'In the museum in Myohyangsan they have another train wagon, a gift from Mao Zedong,' she adds. 'We will visit this museum this afternoon.'

On the wall next to the train is a map with all the countries Kim Il-sung visited by train and plane: the Soviet Union, China, Eastern Europe, West Africa and south-east Asia feature heavily. There was still a lot to travel in the world when a sizeable chunk was still communist. On one side Kim's train-wagon windows can be looked through into the interior, which is all velvet in clashing colours, with Mao-style armchairs. In the next room is Kim Il-sung's Mercedes S-Class Guard W140. It's black and looks brand new. The tires and the front screen are bulky because they are bullet-proof – a fact also shown by the wider wheel arches, which carry the heavy load.

After that, there is an Honours Room. It's a large collection of decorations and ordinary medals mainly from communist and tyrannical nations. Some of the medals look as if they were bought from the gift shop of a struggling provincial museum. It must have been quite a blow when all these 'friends' turned capitalist and started shunning their erstwhile ally. The North Korean media chose not to mention the revolutions that overthrew the other communist dictatorships when they took place.

And all of this is copied downstairs! Down the very grand

staircase we go, through the largest entrance hall I have ever seen. There is another dust-blowing machine (is this in case the previous one didn't do the job properly, or does one need to be extra clean for Kim II?), and then we march into Kim Jong-il's mummy room. It's a replica of his father's, and we are subjected to the same protocol. By the time he was in charge (1994–2011) the list of countries where the red carpet was rolled out for communist tyrants had shrunk substantially. Kim II had to do without Eastern Europe, for example. The interior of his train wagon is in 1980s boat style, with blonde wood and blue carpets. There is a laptop computer on his desk: as one of the happy few who were allowed internet in the country, he was a keen surfer. We know this because in 2001 he asked US Secretary of State Madeleine Albright for her email address; and in 2002 he said he loved surfing South Korean websites. North Korea's Ministry of Truth described him as 'an internet expert'.

Kim II enjoyed a fleet of six personal trains, made up of ninety armoured wagons. All the Kims' secret palaces can be reached by train. His personal trains travelled in groups of three: the first to check the safety of the line; the second one, passing between twenty and sixty minutes later, carried the Great Leader; and the third one carried the minions. Security measures were increased after the 2004 Ryongchon incident when a train exploded three hours after Kim Jong-il's train had passed by. It was huge: all buildings within 1.5km of the explosion were destroyed; the Red Cross estimated that this amounted to some 1,800 houses. Mobile phones were briefly banned, as it was thought that a bomb had been detonated by phone.

Kim Jong-il died on his train during a domestic trip. It was claimed that he suffered a heart attack when he heard that there had been a major defect at a crucial hydroelectric dam. It is certainly possible: what with creating one of the largest famines in Asian history and overseeing the total collapse of the economy, Kim II's nerves must have been under severe strain.

Today, for Kim Jong-un, private trains no longer suffice. He is the proud owner of a 53m Soviet Ilyushin IL-62 jet, which, as I mentioned earlier, has been dubbed 'Air Force Un'. The plane could easily carry 200 people but is used exclusively by the Great Leader and his unpurged aides. One of his favourite ways of impressing his top brass is to take them for a spin above the capital to see the building projects, or, as he puts it, to 'showcase the level of civilisation of the Koreans and the mental power of the army and people'. Satellite photos have shown that Kim Jong-un had a number of private airfields constructed next to his secret palaces.

Kim II's Honours Room is less impressive than his father's. Not to fall short, Kim Jong-il gave himself a long list of titles. Many referred to his military functions, even though he had never had military training or service. The titles include, among others: Dear Leader; Guiding Sun Ray; Brilliant Leader; Shining Star of Paektu Mountain; Heavenly Leader; Unique Leader; Commander-in-Chief; Fate of the Nation; Sun of the Communist Future; Ever-Victorious, Iron-Willed Commander; Invincible and Triumphant General; Guarantee of the Fatherland's Reunification; Beloved and Respected General; The Great Sun of Life; Guiding Star of the Twenty-First Century; Bright Sun of Juche; Highest

Incarnation of the Revolutionary Comradeship; Glorious General Who Descended From Heaven.

After the Honours Room, it takes another half an hour through endless corridors to leave the palace. We are let loose in the park in front of it. It is suggested we have our group photo taken, and again I dive over so I won't be seen in front of the Kims' tomb.

I am still surprised by the size of this former palace, and decide to be bad.

'Mrs Kim, don't you find it a bit strange that in a country where there is famine, the president built himself such a large palace?'

She looks over my shoulder, as if momentarily distracted, and does not reply.

So I repeat my question.

Mr Chong comes to her aid: 'You don't understand. This is what the people want. The Parliament decided this. It is democratic. We want the president to have this palace.'

Silly me.

A democratic Parliament? When there are elections, there is only one candidate per constituency seat; and each one is put forward by the Democratic Front for the Reunification of the Fatherland. This is a group of three parties led by the Workers' Party of Korea. Of the other parties one never hears anything, apart from the names of their leaders.

On the bus we introduce our minders to *real* democracy.

CHAPTER TWELVE

WHAT DO YOU GIVE A TYRANT
WHO HAS EVERYTHING?

Mrs Kim makes the mistake of saying that we have the choice of seeing the Pyongyang Symphony Orchestra, should we be interested.

At first there is silence.

Then one of the Lithuanians in the back asks:

'How long will it take? I would be interested if it was a short repertoire.'

'I don't know,' Mrs Kim replies. 'I shall find out.'

'Can we see something else?' one of the other guys asks.

'Yes, what are the alternatives?'

'Are there several alternatives? Can we have a vote?' I recognise Kate's voice.

'I'd like to hear the orchestra,' Federico asserts.

'Maybe we can see the circus. Who would like to see the circus instead?' Mrs Kim suggests.

'Do they use animals in the circus?' Italian Edo asks, his voice sounding worried. He sits just behind me.

'Can we see both the circus AND the orchestra?'

'Yes, I am up for that.'

'Me too,' another one shouts.

'If there are animals in the circus, I am not going to the circus,' Edo states.

'Oh no, there are no animals. Just acrobats and clowns,' Mrs Kim reassures him. She looks harassed.

'Is there a third option? For those who neither want to see the circus nor the symphony?' somebody new asks.

'How long will we be at the circus? Could we not go to the symphony today, and the circus tomorrow?' Pete interjects.

Mr Chong, Mrs Kim and American Josh look at each other, despairing.

It does not end there.

'Mrs Kim, on a slightly different subject: the other group is going to the pizza restaurant for lunch. Apparently there is a pizza restaurant here in Pyongyang. Can we go to that today?' one of the Lithuanians now shouts from the back.

'YES PLEASE!' four or five people chime in.

'I vote we go to a pizza restaurant. I've had enough of North Korean food!'

'Yes!'

'PIZZA! PIZZZA! PIZZA!'

'Down with kimchi!'

Guffaws.

'Are there other cuisines we could taste in Pyongyang apart from pizza?'

'It's not that easy. The pizza restaurant is not owned by the KITC travel agency, but by another one,' American minder Josh says, always keen to emphasise difficulties.

'How come?' I ask Josh later. 'I thought KITC was the only North Korean travel agency.'

'No, there are several,' he replies.

'But how come? Are they private?'

'No, they are all owned by the state, but somehow they seem to be competing.'

The pizza referendum debates on the coach are continuing. When the bus stops, Mrs Kim looks relieved.

'This is the Revolutionary Martyrs' Cemetery!' she announces.

Somebody moans in the back.

'You will enjoy it, there is a great view over the city,' trouper Mr Chong announces.

The view on the top of the Daesong Hill must normally be far-reaching, but today it's hazy and a bit pointless. We keep dithering in the fog; perhaps we are ahead of our schedule.

This cemetery is dedicated to the guerrillas who gave their lives fighting for independence from the Japanese. It's an interesting concept as the liberation from the Japanese took place because the Allies won the war against the Axis Powers. That the removal of the Japanese is owed to US and Soviet efforts is never mentioned. There allegedly is a small monument dedicated to the Soviet Union tucked away in a forgotten corner of Pyongyang, but nobody is ever taken there. Nonetheless, many North Koreans perished:

during its colonial occupation the Japanese were so effective in fighting the communist guerrillas that they were all either killed or fled to China.

Incidentally, Kim Il-sung wanted to be buried in this cemetery, too. Kim Jong-il refused this, possibly because he feared that it would bring back reverence for his father's ex-guerrilla mates, who Jong-il had purged to strengthen his own position.

We walk across another huge tiled square towards the monument itself. I descry another statue to bow to and lay flowers at. Change of subject though: this time we are going to show respect to *Mama* Kim. This is a first. Before and after us are smaller groups of North Koreans who not only bow and lay flowers for Mama Kim, but also have their group photo taken.

Kim Jong-suk was the second wife of widower Kim Il-sung, and the mother of Kim II. She was born in 1919 in Japanese-occupied North Korea. Jong-suk moved with her mother to Chinese Manchuria to join her father. Jong-suk joined Kim Il-sung's guerrilla group as a kitchen helper. She was arrested in 1937, and rejoined the guerrillas. According to invented North Korean history she then saved Kim Il-sung's life when six Japanese soldiers ambushed them. She allegedly shielded Kim Il-sung with her body and fired back. The official hagiographer Baik Bong wrote that 'this was not the only time such dangers occurred, and each time, Comrade Kim Jung-suk rose to the occasion with fury, and protected the headquarters of the revolution at the risk of her life'.

Tender love blossomed and, in 1941, Kim Il-sung and Jong-suk married in the village of Vyatskoye in the Soviet Union, possibly because she was pregnant. In 1941 or 1942 Kim II was born there. In 1948 the DPRK was established and Kim Il-sung became Prime Minister and Head of State.

Apart from saving her man's life, invented North Korean history has come up with other heroic stories to legitimise Jong-suk's elevation to Virgin Mary stature. According to North Korean textbooks, Comrade Kim Jong-suk, to support the Respected Leader, made many long and rugged journeys to visit our people and arouse them to the building of a new country. She even put off her visit to her own native town and her own kinsfolk, whom she had never forgotten for even a second in the days of her anti-Japanese struggle.

In other words: she didn't bother visiting her parents. Similar mythical heroic conduct has been attributed to Kim Il-sung himself: on the road to his ancestral home at Mangyongdae is a monument where he halted to decide whether to go and visit them after all those years, or go and give some on-the-spot guidance to factory workers. He heroically chose the latter.

Kim Jong-suk washed Kim Il-sung's socks and dried them on her bosom.

Near Kungang Mountain (the most beautiful mountain in the world according to North Koreans) there is a monument where Jong-suk stopped, realised she hadn't brought lunch for the Great Leader, and turned back to prepare something.

Once upon a time there was a violent snowstorm in the valley of the Sobaek. The first heroic deed occurred when Kim Jong-suk put an army blanket on baby Kim II. When it proved still too cold, she took off her own cotton-quilted coat and covered the baby with it. Now Kim was shivering, and 'the women guerrillas' hearts ached'. They all searched for bits of cloth to make a patchwork quilt. One woman even donated a piece of cotton she had received from Kim Jong-suk for her birthday and which 'she had kept in her rucksack even in the days of heavy fighting!' A West-German Kim groupie went all lyrical about this momentous sacrifice: 'A quilt that has cost millions of gold coins cannot be compared to that patched quilt, the crystallisation of the warm hearts of the anti-Japanese women guerrillas who held Kim Jong-il as the guiding sun.' One cannot help but wonder why Kim Jong-suk did not catch pneumonia while her mates were beavering away at the patchwork quilt.

One day Kim Jong-suk visited the committee for organising the Women's Union in North Hamgyong Province. An official apologised for the state of their offices. She reassured Kim that the chairwoman, the vice-chairwoman and department heads would eventually be provided with proper swivel chairs. Kin Jong-suk was offered one of the only two swivel chairs they had already obtained. And lo! Kim Jong-suk reprimanded them, and said 'that they should not take on airs with swivel chairs; that mixing with the masses was more important than a comfortable office!' She then took a seat on a wooden chair and said: 'I feel more comfortable on such a wooden chair than on the swivel chair.'

The reality of Kim Jong-suk's life is slightly less prosaic: during the less than one year as First Lady she was completely unknown. She died in 1949, according to invented North Korean history, 'as a consequence of the suffering she endured while fighting the Japanese'. In the real world, it is thought that she died in childbirth or from tuberculosis.

When Kim Jong-il became the heir apparent in 1974, the unknown Jong-suk suddenly became 'a great communist guerrilla' care of the propaganda machine. A statue and museum were built in her home town. When Kim Il-sung died, Kim Jong-il transformed his mother into the third leg of the North Korean Holy Trinity. Kim Il-sung, Kim Jong-il and Jong-suk are now known locally as 'the Three Generals of Paektu Mountain.'* In 1980, Mama Kim was given the title 'Mother of Korea'. In the 1990s Jong-suk's portrait started to be added to those of Kim Il-sung and Kim Jong-il, and equally treated as a holy relic.

Back on the bus, Mrs Kim announces with sadness in her voice that we will, after all, not visit the International Friendship Exhibition Hall. I am annoyed because my friend Alex, who visited North Korea last year, had said that it was an absolute must, and one of the most bizarre places he went to while here.

The Exhibition Hall is a magnificent 150-room museum in the untouched biosphere of Mount Myohyang, a two-hour drive north from Pyongyang. Well, not entirely untouched, as the dictatorship has thought fit to defile one entire mountain side with the inscription 'KIM JONG-IL, IRON-WILLED COMMANDER'. Mount Myohyang was the favourite place of Kim Il-sung and also hides

---

* This is based on the fabrication that they somehow lived in a 'Secret Camp' on Paektu Mountain, when Kim Jong-il was born. As we have seen earlier, they lived in Russia when Jong-il was born.

one of the Kims' many palaces. Tourists are taken to visit Kim Il-sung's underground bunker there. The soldiers at the entrance carry silver AK47s; the soldiers inside carry gold ones. My friend described it as distinctly scary.

The International Friendship Exhibition Hall (a bit of a misnomer in the case of North Korea) above it houses 200,000 gifts that the Kims received from foreign despots, communists, terrorist regimes and random celebrities. What do you give the discerning tyrant who already has everything?

The marble halls covered by green pagoda roofs include: a stuffed crocodile, sitting up straight, carrying a wooden tray with wooden cocktail glasses and matching ashtray from the Sandinistas in Nicaragua; a basketball signed by Michael Jordan from US Ambassador Madeleine Albright; chess boards from Gaddafi; a gem-encrusted sword from Chairman Arafat of the impoverished Palestinian Authority; silver chopsticks from Mongolia; and a bullet-proof limousine from Stalin. Cambodian King Norodom Sihanouk spent much of his exile in a palace in North Korea. His gifts include a painting of a broom sweeping an American soldier off a map of south-east Asia.

Spare a thought for the machine gun from Poland and the dagger and revolver sent by former East German leader Honecker, as if to kit out a bandit. The Chairman of the Journalist Association of Kuwait showed his deep appreciation by way of a pen set. The Hwabei Tire Factory of China sent a tiny rubber ashtray.

But let us pause for a second by one of the Leaders' most treasured gifts: a bear's head on a red satin pillow received from Nicolae

Ceaușescu of Romania. Ceaușescu was the Kims' best friend.* After his visit to North Korea in 1971, Nicolae and Elena decided to copy the North Korean model of total state authority and tyrant personality cult. Like so many other second-rate leaders, Ceaușescu declared his reforms a 'Third Way', which would soon be copied elsewhere.

There were many parallels between the two countries. During the Christmas revolution, which toppled the Ceaușescus in 1989, it even transpired that there existed a secret network of tunnels underneath Bucharest to allow security services to get around during trouble – just like the rumoured secret metro in Pyongyang.

---

* Ceaușescu built up a reputation as an independent communist when he condemned the invasion of Czechoslovakia by the Warsaw Pact countries in 1968. In the West this turned him into a hero overnight. Initially many Romanians, including non-communists, responded enthusiastically to his call to take up arms in case the Warsaw Pact should attempt to invade Romania as well.

He could use his grandstanding against the Soviet Union only for so long though: he needed the USSR's material aid. He now searched for another way in which to enthuse the Romanians into supporting him. He found the solution when he brought a one-week visit to North Korea in 1971.

He was mightily impressed by the extreme forms of adulation the Pyongyang regime organised for itself. During the visit Kim Il-sung even forced his population to wear badges with Ceaușescu's face.

As soon as Ceaușescu returned to Romania he announced a dramatic overhaul of policies to line them up with those of his new friends in East Asia. Control over education, culture and mass media was centralised under the aegis of the Communist Party; propaganda was dramatically expanded by way of re-education and mass cultural movements; a new ideology was invented by merging Marxism-Leninism with Romanian nationalism; and a new personality cult was launched. Only the genius *Conducator* could centrally plan towards ever greater prosperity and defend the people against alien invaders.

Ceaușescu's regime also copied the more idiosyncratic aspects of the regime in Pyongyang: he had all references to his life rewritten for propaganda purposes; his birthplace was rebuilt and opened as a shrine to the public; he had his own 'National Museum of Gifts to the Ceaușescus' set up; and he built himself a palace that is one of the world's largest buildings (the rooms were so vast that it is impossible to heat them – icicles hang from the ceilings in winter). In one aspect the Ceaușescus went even further than the Kims: Elena Ceaușescu had herself awarded a PhD in Chemistry from the University of Bucharest notwithstanding the fact that she had not attended high school. Whenever they went on official visits she also demanded Honorary Degrees from prestigious universities and became very angry at 'Mr Peanut', when President Carter of the United States told her he could not obtain an Honorary Degree from the University of Washington for her. The Kims never appear to have tried that.

The museum must show the North Koreans that their leaders are universally acclaimed. It does not explain that the exchange of gifts is a diplomatic custom.

Excitement is mounting: we are off to the pizza restaurant!

CHAPTER THIRTEEN

THE LEADERS LOVE
THEIR FLOWERS

Svelte modern apartment-blocks in terracotta, blue and white line the Mirae Scientists' Street. It was opened only last year. The flats were built for scientists and academic staff from the Kim Chaek University of Technology. One building in which the North Korean authorities take particular pride is a 53-floor electric-blue tower resembling an upturned wheat spikelet.

'This building was built in just six months!' Mrs Kim marvels through the coach's microphone.

'Our Great Leader Kim Jong-un said that if one wants to see what North Korea is truly like, people should come to Mirae Scientists' Street. He said that the apartments prove the superiority of the North Korean socialist system because humble educators and scientists live here for free without paying rent.'

Well. Under the North Korean state housing allocation system, the educators and scientists have no choice. They are commanded to live here. Notwithstanding a lot of not-so-soft pressure, many refuse to move in, because all is not well in Mirae Scientists' Street.

According to the South Korean *North Korea Daily*, when Kim Jong-un opened the complex he was shown only the few apartments that were actually finished. Most flats remain shells to this day. The apartments' heating doesn't work, so last winter the radiators froze solid. The electricity is not properly supplied yet. The water mains connections are wonky, too; and the residents have been ordered not to use the lifts if they live below the tenth floor.

But all this is nothing compared to the people's main fear: shoddy construction. The building of the Scientists' Street apartments started with master builder Kim Jong-un's on-the-spot-guidance in May 2014. In February 2015 Kim suddenly announced that the first phase was to be completed by April, and the second by October. The around-the-clock speed building this necessitated produced a half-finished scheme. Apart from the absent electricity, water and heating supply, where else were corners cut? In the structure of the building itself, apparently. In May 2014, a 23-storey apartment-block nearby collapsed and hundreds were killed. Who is surprised that the recipients of the state's munificence refuse to move in?

After the collapse, in good old North Korean fashion, Deputy Minister for Construction Choe Yong-gon was executed by a simple firing squad.

Choe Yong-gon was lucky: three months earlier Defence Chief Hyon Yong-chol was executed by putting him in front of an anti-aircraft gun. Officially, he had committed the crime of falling asleep during a military rally attended by Kim Jong-un; rumour had it that in reality he had refused to carry out one of Kim's orders. That would put the number of senior officials who were purged and executed since Kim came to power four years earlier at seventy.

You may wonder on what basis so many individuals are being executed in North Korea. Is it by law, or at the Leader's say-so? Like almost every other human right, the right to life (arguably the most important one) does not exist in the pariah state. Even though under international treaties to which North Korea is a signatory the death penalty can be considered only for the most heinous crimes, in North Korea it is just another routine punishment. Under North Korean criminal law it is applied for theft, counterfeiting currency, escaping from prison, operating a private business and other unspecified 'serious crimes'. It can also be applied when no remorse is shown.

On top of this, a raft of public bodies has also decided to introduce the death penalty for other crimes such as exchanging foreign currency. Defectors witnessed public executions for siphoning off rice, possessing a bible, and helping people to flee to the South. In theory a fair trial is provided; in reality summary executions without an actual trial take place quite often. They usually happen in concentration camps. Sometimes the executions are in public, whereby, for example, the accused's work unit or people living in the vicinity are told to attend and watch.

The Ryung Song Italy Pizza Restaurant is up a flight of stairs in one of the apartment buildings in Mirae Scientists' Street. I heard from a friend that sometimes you have to wait for half an hour until the electricity comes back on. Today everything is brightly lit. We sit with twelve people at a round table. Elevator music is playing in the background. The pizza is passable, but for some reason you have to pay an extra two dollars (US) to add cheese.

The history of pizza making in North Korea is another Kim-esque story. Kim II craved pizza, so in the 1990s he instructed his ambassador in Italy to select Italian pizza chefs to come and teach a number of army officers how to do it. The chefs were interviewed by several North Korean diplomats, and those selected were told that they would leave in fifteen days. They were paid in advance with cash in brown envelopes and had to draft up a list of the ingredients they needed. Once they arrived in Pyongyang, the chefs and their wives had their passports confiscated, and they were housed in one of the marble presidential palaces. The men were then subjected to brain scans, blood and urine sampling and X-rays, 'so there wouldn't be any problems'. Eventually the chefs taught a few soldiers how to make pizza. Used to instructions rather than to autonomous thinking, one of the soldiers asked chef Ermanno Furlanis what the distance should be between the olives on the pizza. Unfortunately, what the soldiers came up with tasted too much like military canteen food, so Kim instigated a new plan. He now sent a number of North Koreans to Italy to learn the tricks of the trade in situ. This proved more successful, and in March 2009 the first pizza restaurant opened in Pyongyang.

This presumably encouraged Kim to introduce hamburgers to North Korea as well. He ordered that a factory be built. North

Korean call burgers *gogigyeopbbang*, which means 'double bread with meat'. North Koreans now believe that Kim invented the hamburger. The Ministry of Truth could of course not tell the people that it is American: only evil comes out of the imperialists' country. In the state media, Coca-Cola is translated as 'cesspool water of American capitalism'.

Tired of the endless bottles of beer, I order a bottle of North Korean red wine. I am joined in this enterprise by my friend Hong Kong Edward. It tastes like fortified grape juice and is very sweet, but, contrary to the group's gloomy and laconic predictions, it didn't give me a headache the next day. Two waitresses start singing karaoke, but people just look bored or go on talking to others, and after two songs they give up. None of the waiters seems able to make individual decisions, and when you ask for something, a second one is always called upon to double check the decision process.

Then there is an incident.

One by one, or in pairs or small groups, we leave the restaurant and walk towards the coach. I'm on my own, and I walk towards the spot where the coach dropped us off about two blocks down the road. I find myself admiring the relative beauty of Mirae Scientists' Street. There is still a faint whiff of fresh concrete. The air is dry and crisp.

I feel rather self-conscious, as I'm the only non-Korean. I suddenly realise that my travel companions are nowhere to be seen. I can't remember in which exact side street the coach dropped us off. I try the second one and the third one. No coach. Was it further down? I walk some more blocks. I look behind me, and can see none from our group. I haven't got my glasses on, maybe that's why.

So I walk back to the pizza restaurant.

But now I can't find it any more! It was upstairs in a residential block, and from the outside you couldn't see the commercial activity that was going on inside.

I hasten my steps. I walk back to the second and third side streets, and venture further in them: perhaps the coach is parked around the corner at the end of the side street?

But the coach is nowhere to be seen.

I wonder what to do. Will they come and look for me? If only I could find the pizza restaurant – the people from the restaurant can probably reach Mrs Kim by phone.

I ask a few locals for the pizza restaurant. None of them speaks English. One woman with excessive make-up who seems to be a receptionist at the entrance of a building replies something in Korean, but I cannot understand one word of it. Dejected, I walk back into the street.

Come to think of it, I could not even hail a taxi as there are no taxis to hail and I couldn't explain where to go to.

I start thinking that perhaps I should walk back to the hotel. After all, I am in a street that runs parallel to the river. So if I walk upstream, I am bound to arrive at the bridge that leads to the island where my hotel is – unless I am arrested beforehand. That might actually be a way out, as they would no doubt bring me back. Genius, or what?

Then I see Mr Chong running towards me, hands waving, panic in his eyes.

My friend, Hong Kong Edward, continues the story:

Everybody was on the coach, and it departed. Mrs Kim grabbed the microphone as per usual, and asked whether we had eaten well. We had! We were all very satisfied that we had voted to go to a pizza restaurant instead of one more kimchi-joint.

'Is everybody here?' Mrs Kim then asked, distractedly, while the coach set off.

She was not expecting anybody to be missing. She started counting us, though, but as you know, she always miscounts so she has to do it several times. Then I realised you weren't there! So I raised the alarm.

The coach came to a screeching halt; we all fell forward. Mr Chong was as pale as a sheet. The door of the coach opened, and even before the coach had come to a full stop, Mr Chong jumped out, and ran and ran, as if his life depended upon it. He was panicking. We had never seen him in such a state.

Well yes, perhaps his life would have depended upon finding me. It is well known that if foreigners cause trouble, their minders are punished. And poor Mr Chong was only on his first trip as a minder! He must have been petrified – he would at least have lost his job.

Once I am on the coach, we are hurried to the Pyongyang Circus. Not all of us: Edo and Federico have chosen to attend the guaranteed animal-free Pyongyang Symphony Orchestra. The two of them are sent on their way in a separate coach.

The circus is a permanent concrete building and is very grand, like all official buildings here.

'In the past, some of the acts have won the circus competition in Monte Carlo,' Mrs Kim says.

I wonder whether she has any idea what Monte Carlo is like.

We are put among the locals in the lower tier of the circus, with the ring right in front of us. It starts off with a lady in national dress breathlessly shouting high-pitched slogans. I can hear the names of the Leaders several times. This is interrupted by applause.

I have read that occasionally they put up acts with bears – and that the bears look very thin, possibly because they have been mistreated to be able to perform the acts. Some have suggested that the bears may in fact be humans in a bear suit. I cannot tell, as there are none today. There are trapeze artists, acrobats and two clowns who joke to each other in Korean. I never saw the point of clowns.

'Do you think they are joking about the Kims?' I ask Hong Kong Edward.

Half-way through the acts we have to leave to go to the Mass Dance, and so we climb over the seats in the dark. I had never been to a circus before, but French Céline says the acts were old-fashioned.

In front of a monumental building from where the Kims are watching us from above a slogan saying 'Comrade Kim Il-sung and Comrade Kim Jong-il will be with us forever', perhaps one thousand couples are dancing to music from giant loudspeakers.

The women wear national hoop-dresses, the men black suits and white shirts.

'Mrs Kim, where do they all come from? Are they members of a dance club?'

She hesitates for a moment.

'They are just from around here, from the neighbourhood.'

As if they are just having an impromptu meet-up for a *kaffee-klatsch*. A few hundred foreigners observe the phenomenon from the steps of the building. Some join in. Most dance disjointedly; the Koreans do not look amused. It is impossible to ascertain whether that is because of their inadequate dancing partners, or because they are there against their will. Or maybe their blood boils when they see eager foreigners joining in the dance for the greater glory of the beloved Leader?

No North Korean would mistake these gatherings for anything else than rehearsals for one of the mass events such as Kim Il-sung's birthday, the Arirang Festival or the Pyongyang Gathering of One Million. Some naive tourists still believe this mass dance is solely put on for their amusement. The national holidays when mass events are held, with hundreds of thousands dancing in unison to hail the Great Leaders, require ample prep throughout the year. Attendance at Kim cult events is mandatory. Internally, there is fierce competition between government bodies to outdo each other in extravagance during any celebration of the Kims.

The strange spectacle goes on for about one hour. The colourful dresses turn and whirl; the men in black sweat; the music is joyful. Then suddenly: silence. Inexplicably, all the North Koreans stand in rows and lines as if in a parade ground. Lo and behold, a few of the squares that consist exclusively of men march off in formation. They must be soldiers in civvies. Or maybe not. The regime makes concerted efforts to keep all of society militarised. Even school children and students are made to march in battle formation for roll call in the school yard.

Here at the mass dance, nobody is smiling.

We soon perceive the difference between forced and free-willed activity, when we visit the Moranbong Park in central Pyongyang. The Moranbong Park is not to be confused with the Moranbong *Band*: a North Korean all-female guitar-slinging rock group whose members were carefully selected by Kim Jong-un himself. They perform pop, rock and fusion. In downtown Pyongyang they are fashion outliers. Well, they used to be: their high heels and mini-skirts were perceived as too risqué for the tender feelings of the populace, and have been quietly ditched. When they are not en-tertaining model farmers and exemplary factory workers, they perform for the army. On those occasions they wear military dress, with olive-coloured uniforms featuring epaulettes, knee-high boots and skirts just an inch shorter than the army regulations permit.

The Moranbong Band is intended to compete with South Korean rock groups. The old bands, like the Wangjaesan Light Music Band, the Pochonbo Electronic Ensemble and the Sea of Blood Opera Company, founded by his dad Kim Jong-il, are now old hat. The Unhasu Orchestra has disappeared altogether.

The Moranbong Band's debut concert in 2012 was aimed at inspiring textile workers. They brought a medley of plagiarised

Western *schlagers* and Disney tunes. Their own repertoire includes such light arrangements as 'O My Motherland Full of Hope', 'We Think of the Marshal Day and Night', 'We Can't Live without His Care', 'Fluttering Red Flag' and a song to praise Kim Jong-un: 'We Will Travel to Paektu Mountain'. When they went off-radar for six months it was rumoured that they were enjoying the sights at a concentration camp. But they duly returned. This is not unusual: it happens quite often that South Korean media announces that this or that general has been liquidated by the regime, only for the said general to return from death a few months later.

How successful this attempt is to provide more *circenses* for the population, nobody knows, as polling is not a known pursuit in this hermit tyranny. But the Kims enjoy the Moranbong Band, and they are often seen clapping and laughing from their front-row seats. And that's all that counts.

But this is the park, not the band: lots of ordinary North Koreans are strolling about, chatting, eating ice lollies bought from ladies digging them up from deep inside domestic ice-boxes. They also sell some biscuits and sandwiches: all portable, just in case they need to do a runner when an unbribed official turns up. These are the first private shops we see! Perhaps I ought to report this to the guys behind the Index of Economic Freedom, which ranks North Korea 178th out of 178 countries – it may make them step up by one place or so. I feel compelled to buy something to do my bit to encourage capitalism. We pay in Chinese renminbi; the trade is fast and friendly and ten seconds later I am licking my delicious chocolate ice lolly.

There are some picturesque rocks and little lakes, and amorous couples take photos of each other. But they don't touch: North Koreans are prudish. That said, the marketisation that started after the famine with people trying to make money to buy food in whatever way they can, is allegedly also providing services of the more 'daring' kind. Housewives renting out their homes by the hour to couples who want a quick frolic are not uncommon.

The park is hilly and further up in the privacy of the bushes families are having a picnic. With 10 million out of 24 million malnourished, one wonders what their lunch-boxes contain. Fluorescent kimchi would be my wild guess.

And here in the park the people are dancing too! But this is the difference: they are not in national dress or suits; the music comes from a small CD player instead of huge megaphones; and the dancers are of all ages, but mostly elderly ladies. They smile and look happy. No, this is definitely not the state-run Mass Dance. Besides, it is the first time we are at a spot with many locals present where the Kims are not watching us. The people are dancing in several spots: one particularly beautiful place is at a pavilion with red pillars and a copper-green pagoda roof. The cherry trees are bursting with white blooms and about two hundred people are swirling happily under the milky sky. In fact, it's packed. We hang around for a little while. When I walk a wide circle around the dancers to take a photo from a prettier angle, minder Chong runs towards me and grabs my arm and pulls me back to the group.

'You must stay with group, Mr JP,' he says. 'Do not run away again!'

In the parking lot where the coach is, a wedding party has

arrived. The bride is in national hoop-dress; the groom is in a bizarre suit in light-blue and yellow polyester.

'I came to this park too, to have wedding photos taken,' Mrs Kim unexpectedly reveals. 'In the dress I am wearing now.'

'When did you marry?' I ask.

'Eight years ago.' Her eyes sparkle. Keeping in mind that her father was allowed to come and live in Pyongyang and that she is a minder for foreign tourists and therefore a party member, Mrs Kim must have been a bit of a catch. Until the 1970s, most marriages were arranged by the parents; nowadays love-marriages are common. Nobody here will marry without parental consent, though. Where previously any person working in powerful departments such as the National Security Agency would have been desirable, that is now much less the case as many earn a substantial part of their income in the illegal markets.

We find our driver behind the coach, where he is playing a home-made board game with a fellow driver. Both are sitting on their haunches. It seems like a mixture of backgammon and draughts. The pieces are re-used plastic bottle capsules in different colours.

We visit the annual International Kimilsungia and Kimjongilia Flower Exhibition in its purpose-built halls. Kim Il-sung had a beautiful purple orchid named after him by Sukarno, the erstwhile communist president of Indonesia. Kim Jong-il had to do with a vulgar red begonia on steroids, care of a Japanese horticultural-ist called Kamo Mototeru. The fact that the horticulturalists who grew these flower varieties are foreign is portrayed as evidence that the leaders enjoy worldwide appeal. Or, as the Ministry of Truth phrases it in the Encyclopaedia of Kimjongilia: 'This is a representation of reverence for the exploits Kim Jong-il accumulated for the cause of independence of humanity and also a reflection of the feelings of the Korean people and of the world's progressive people.'*

We have arrived at the end of the day, so the queues are not hundreds of metres long as we were promised. According to the Ministry of Truth, hundreds of thousands of North Korean visit this exhibition annually. Some sources whisper that they are aiming for one million. It must be wonderful selling tickets when the entire workforce of every sector of industry is subject to compulsory attendance.

Each one of the fifty or so stands consists of a tower of Kimilsungias and Kimjongilias. Some other flowers are thrown in for good measure: two proud tulips might, say, peep out of ten pansies. Elsewhere, a gorgeous dissident azalea is trying to break the Kimilsungia landslide. Here and there are single tables with one or two well-tended and stunning plants: perhaps these are private entrants? By and large, it's a gaudy and hilarious affair. In the fore-back or middle ground the flowers are always chaperoned by a maquette of the Juche Tower; the Kims' Mausoleum; the symbol of the Korean Workers' Party; Kim Il-sung's birthplace; or just photos of the Leaders, with or without cute little missiles to fill up

---

* You can buy the Kindle version on Amazon. Its entry contains this little gem: 'The history of flowers of is even longer than that of humanity, and during that time, their numerous species have flourished and emerged around all corners of the globe. However none are more revered and adored by the people than that of Kimjongilia which was named after the great man.'

empty space. It's a competition, and for no apparent reason, some stands have obtained first, second or third prize. Some stands are entirely in the dark as there are not enough light spots available. The stands are designed and paid for by sectors of industry, e.g. the state railways or the state tourist industry or the state farms. My amazement is huge when I spot a stand that has not only been paid for by Cuba, but also by Unicef and the European Union.

Families have their photos taken against a background of one of the stands or a giant photo of the Leader. The hall is now semi-dark as the sun has set and the lighting is insufficient. We've been told that during the day the whole circus is enlivened with strident marching music.

The queue for the loo is too long and we are in a hurry for the next event, which we are told 'is a surprise'. So Mrs Kim takes us to the WC used by the stand keepers. We snake behind a velvet curtain where we encounter the real North Korea.

The loo is filthy. There are puddles on the floor. The silence is broken by the drip, drip, drip from a leak in the cracked concrete ceiling. The besmirched taps don't work. The urinals have never been cleaned. In the corner stands a tub, the size of a bath, filled to the brim with water. What is it for? We saw something similar in the WC of a restaurant yesterday. Only later it dawns on me that this must be a water reserve. The Pyongyang water supply is intermittent; sometimes because of shortages, sometimes because the ancient pipes have burst.

It's already getting dark when we are rushed off to Kim Il-sung Square. Red Square in Moscow was the model, and it is the thirty-seventh largest square in the world. Signs and numbers are painted on the concrete paving slabs so the participants know where to stand and in which direction to move during the mass parades.

In prime position is a granite construction similar to Lenin's mausoleum. This is the terrace from where the Leader can observe the troops, the mass dances and the parades. Behind it is the towering building of the Grand Study House with its pretty pagoda roofs. The official buildings lining the square sport large banners featuring strappy workers and slogans in red. Except for the propaganda signs, the vast square is sparsely lit. They have made a good effort to point the lights straight into people's eyes in order to blind them. According to Mrs Kim there are often torchlight processions here. I've asked to attend one, but my requests remain unheeded and unacknowledged.

Large streams of people are marching towards the square, but they somehow do not venture to the central part where the foreigners have been told to wait for the fireworks. Most locals seem to have gathered near the river; perhaps for a better view.

Loud bangs herald the start of the fireworks. They are being set off from behind the Juche Tower.

The fireworks are grand and spatter the night sky with brilliant reds. Passing overcrowded buses slow down to allow the driver a view, thereby blocking out the view of the audience massed on the other side, who protest loudly and shake their fists.

Oh, and there is grand marching music over the speaker system, of course.

Everybody is knackered but our minders are not letting up. Perhaps they take our tiredness for capitalist slacking. North Korean propaganda states that capitalists 'only want the easy life'. Heaven forbid!

Now we are dragged off to another one of the KITC restaurants. It's an indoor BBQ again, of a different type from the previous ones. My heart sinks, because there are never extractors in these places and therefore our clothes will stink and there is no opportunity to wash them. It's a protracted affair and the food is nothing special, as per usual. The meat consists mainly of boiled fat.

We are then asked to sit in a circle around a TV to watch Kim Kubrick's video of our past few days. After about fifteen minutes he starts to fast-forward his masterpiece. I suspect it's not going to be shortlisted for the Oscars just yet: he does not know the meaning of editing and the footage of every monument we've attended is endless; adding up to two-and-a-half hours in total. Also, this is just the standard film made for about ten groups or so; most of the time the images do not show us, but complete strangers; as well as monuments we didn't visit. At sixty euros a pop, I pass. Sadly I do feature in it, as I tend to walk ahead of the group and, without editing, I am often the first person one sees at every new Kim-site.

We conclude the evening by eating a passable birthday cake made for French Céline.

'You are so lucky, having been born on the birthday of the Great Leader Kim Il-sung!' Mrs Kim cries.

We are all a bit downcast and apprehensive, as tomorrow we will depart from this strange country. We know that there is a risk of trouble with the notoriously strict North Korean border guards.

CHAPTER FOURTEEN

HIDING MEMORY CARDS
IN BREAD ROLLS

The train leaves Pyongyang Station at 10 a.m. Most of our group left at 4 a.m. by plane. Leaving by train or plane was our individual choice; except for American Natasha. Americans are not allowed to leave North Korea by train. Imagine all the militarily sensitive potato fields they might photograph from the windows!

The few of us who are leaving by train are joined by the remnants of four other groups; and we are all stowed together in one first-class wagon. The other fifteen wagons are empty. The North Korean authorities are not going to run the risk of their citizens mingling with foreigners on a train. Over the border in China, a number of other foreigners will board but they will travel second class, and at night the doors to our first-class wagon are locked with a chain and padlock. To go to the restaurant car the padlock has to be unlocked by our *trainführer* who does not speak one word of English. It is unclear whether he is North Korean or Chinese. What is also unclear is at what end of the train the restaurant car is, and so my friend Edward and I walk the length of ten wagons before we turn around and try the other direction. We never find the restaurant car.

But I am running ahead of myself. I am sharing our four-berth compartment with Hong Kong Edward from my group. At his suggestion we take the low berths, as these will allow us to lie down during the day without bumping our heads against the ceiling, as in the upper berths. We are hoping that nobody else will join us, but every compartment is to be fully stowed, so two complete strangers are pushed in by the *trainführer*: another Hong Kong-Chinese, and an Australian who says he is 'in publishing' and then proceeds to give secret winks to make us believe that he is a writer or a journalist. By now I am a bit blasé about the excessive secretiveness and suspicions of some of my fellow travellers.

From the platform Mrs Kim and Mr Chong wave at our dirty windows. The train sets into motion, and they shrink until we can see them no more.

Do they believe the propaganda they told us? How will we ever know? Their faces were masks at all times. Any North Korean would have to be completely bonkers to risk the concentration camp for a few whispered confidences to a foreigner. Over eight days, you do get some idea as to what your minders are like, of course. Our two seemed more human than the two minders of our 'shadow' group. After a few days, Mrs Kim loosened up – probably when she realised that we were responsible people who would not cause her too much trouble. As far as I know none of us tried to elicit unlawful utterances from our minders or anybody we met; and, more likely than not, they would inform on us if we had done so. To some degree I was even careful with my fellow travellers: how can you be 100 per cent certain that one in the group is not a plant? For a regime obsessed with security, it would be an obvious move.

These are our last hours in North Korea and everybody is on edge. We have all heard the stories of people being arrested and dragged off the plane or train just when they were about to leave the country. None of us wants to be left behind in the gulag. We have been told that the border officers will be thorough. Only now do I hear that those flying can expect only a perfunctory search, but that *we* will get the Full Monty. So many titbits of practical information about North Korea come through too late by way of gossipy whispers.

It's photo-memory-card-hiding-time.

As we have been told before we arrived and almost daily since then, there are heaps of subjects that are officially *verboten* to photograph. Therefore you self-censure. Inexorably, every time you take a photo of a perilous subject you wonder: is this worth being thrown in prison for? Almost invariably it isn't. So you don't take the photo. But sometimes the subject is too good to let it pass. Edward, my travel friend, has been taking photos non-stop since we arrived in North Korea, and has almost 1,000 of them on two memory cards. He also made films with his small, anonymous, white camera.

'I will hide one memory card behind the bench,' he announces, twinkles in his eyes. He puts something behind his headrest.

I now wonder: should he have told me this? What if they

interrogate me and pull my finger nails out with dirty surgical instruments? Could I keep his secret?

I end up pushing a memory card inside the little bread roll I bought at the train station. I must remember not to eat it.

All over the train wagon similar scenes are occurring. Nobody is walking around; nobody is chatting; everybody is trembling for the border inspection.

There are two other reasons why it is quiet though. Many went on a big night out and are suffering from the after-effects. On top of that, it is positively tropical. The thermometer in the corridor reads 28 degrees. Unhelpfully, there are stickers on the windows stating in English that it is forbidden to open the windows. When I open one I am berated by the *trainführer*. With hand gestures I try to make clear that it is too hot and that the windows should be opened. He shrugs. He probably thinks that I, as a 'pampered tourist, should be kept warm thanks to the regime'. It's ungrateful for the foreigner to reject his privileged position. As I said before, excessive heat is a North Korean 'thing'. It comes with having grown up in unheated houses where the cow forgotten outside froze to death.

The tension is palpable. Will there be an incident at the border? Will one of us be arrested? I am mainly concerned about my diary, which I hope they will not take off me. I have bought a dodgy-looking one-litre carton of Argentinian wine in the hotel shop for four dollars, but Edward and I agree that we will not start drinking until we have passed the border. If anything, I don't want to be drunk if I am to be interrogated with strong lights pointed at my eyes!

The thought occurs that it might be a good idea to fatten up just in case I get arrested. So I pass the remainder of the time eating the leftover food I turned my nose up at before.

I hope that once I have left North Korea, the sneezing will be gone. For the past eight days I have been sneezing and blowing my nose incessantly. Pyongyang means 'City of Willows', and I am allergic to willow trees. I am allergic to North Korea.

The undulating landscape under the milky-white sky is tiresome. Treeless plains with clay-coloured earth and whitewashed villages blink past the windows. Occasionally you see congregations of locals working like ants in the barren fields. Then we reach the border. Suddenly the train is enveloped by walls and very high fences.

We come to a shrieking halt. It's 3 p.m. We will only leave again at seven, when it's dark already. By then it's also dark in the North Korean town of Sinuiju where we are waiting; while on the other side of the river the Chinese city of Yuanbao is a sea of light from skyscrapers, advertising and twenty-first centuryism. It must be quite something for North Koreans who live on the border to see their faces light up when they look across the river. It's like a megaphone barking: 'You live in poverty. We are rich. Don't believe a word of what your leaders tell you.' Perhaps China is really the country that the Kims hate most, as North Korea's high-ranking defector Jang Jin-sung suggested in his book *Dear Leader*.

Why is there anybody left in North Korea? Surely it should have been empty of people by now?

For the first two decades after independence North Korea didn't do too badly. The Japanese had industrialised the north, and had left the south rural, to serve as a bread basket for Japan. In addition, because of its strategic position, North Korea managed to wrench substantial aid from both China and the Soviet Union. During the famine in China caused by Mao's Great Leap Forward, Koreans from China actually fled to North Korea, where life was better. At the time the regime still managed to keep its people in complete isolation, and so many believed that life was better in North Korea than elsewhere in the world. Why move to South Korea, where 'human rights are violated', 'people live under the jackboot of the American imperialists', 'crime, misery, and poverty are rampant' with 'diseases and homelessness everywhere you look'?

It all started to change in the 1980s when the economy slowed down. But the floodgates really opened in the 1990s when the economy collapsed and central-planning mistakes caused famine. People died in the streets and survival became more important than obeying the tyrants.

The trickle of illegal crossings increased exponentially. The cross-border traffic takes three forms: some go to China to find and buy food, and travel back; others become smugglers, buying goods in China to sell in North Korea; and the third category are the refugees proper – those who have no intention of returning.

North Korea is separated from China and Russia by the Yalu and the Tumen rivers. There are large stretches where you can easily wade to the other side. When the rivers are frozen solid you can walk across. You can pay border guards to show you the direction to walk in, or to look the other way. Becoming a border guard is now a desirable profession as it provides for rich pickings. You can pay for locals to bring you to the other side and to help once you are in China. Where previously being housed at the faraway border was seen as a punishment, it is now perceived as a business opportunity. The levels of service provided by people traffickers range from merely pointing out where to cross to the 'gold star service', which ends when you land in Seoul.

Fake identity papers can be bought, too. And travel permits: there is a long waiting time if you want to do it in the official way, but the queue can be jumped for about US $100. There is a large Korean community living over the border in China, who are also willing to help – or to profit from it. Some single female North Korean defectors willingly or unwillingly end up living with Chinese men, sometimes in virtual slavery.

Sometimes the voyage is paid for by family members who have already reached the South. South Koreans can organise money transfers to their relations to North Korea for a fee of about 30 per cent. They give the money in South Korea to a broker, who transfers it to an account in China. Somebody in North Korea who has a Chinese-bought mobile phone with which he can connect to the Chinese network near the border is told that the money has arrived (this takes some coordinating as many North Koreans who own a Chinese phone prevent tracking by switching their phones on only at pre-arranged times; in addition the dictatorship tries to jam the phones). He then brings the money to the North Korean recipient from the reserves he has in place. Later, money can be smuggled to him from China.

It is risky: if arrested by the Chinese police, you are sent back to North Korea, as China does not recognise North Koreans as political refugees. China is clamping down on illegal entrants, and the police try to smoke them out. The risk is much more severe for high-level North Koreans trying to escape: the North Korean government usually alleges that they are murderers, and will put pressure on the Chinese to find them. It is difficult to assess how many North Koreans live in north-eastern China, as most live there illegally, and keep their heads down. Estimates vary from 20,000 to 100,000.

Immigration to South Korea is the Holy Grail for every North Korean defector. As the countries do not recognise each other as independent nations, but consider the other country an integral part of their own, a North Korean who arrives in Seoul is automatically considered to be a citizen of South Korea. The Ministry of Reunification will cater for his or her needs. They will be debriefed to see whether they are genuine defectors; receive a twelve-week course for social adaptation into South Korean society; receive housing in the area they wish; and receive a settlement support grant. They receive residency support for another five years: this includes vocational training, educational support, social security, subsidised employment, police protection and comprehensive support services through the North Korean Refugees Foundation. They also receive help from a raft of private charities. Sadly, some ex-North Koreans find life in South Korea extremely difficult, and many do not succeed in climbing the socio-economic ladder.

Because of the obstacles in getting to South Korea, not many succeed: in 2014 only 1,396 reached Seoul. The numbers of defectors have been going down in the past ten years or so. From 2009, North Korea's State Security Department tried to clamp down on all avenues of illegal defection. This included tighter surveillance, ideological education, increased travel-permit checks at the borders, tighter inspections at sea, and harsher punishment for those in the border region who are caught using Chinese mobile phones. Following Kim Jong-il's death in 2011, the movement of people became even more tightly controlled. Families living on the border were required to take turns to stand guard. Bed-check inspections by the *inminbans* were increased. It was publicly reiterated that three generations in a family of a defector would be destroyed, and that defectors would be executed on the spot. Authorities threatened to lay land-mines in the border regions. Wire fences, noise censors, devices to detect mobile phones, cameras and camouflaged traps were installed. The border security guards have been told to stop defectors, and if they can't, to shoot them. The market has responded: as the risks have increased, those organising border crossings have increased their fees, as have bribe-taking border guards.

The Korean border guards are all over the train. The doors of our wagon are locked and guarded. The toilets have been locked too. One guy in the next compartment urgently has to go to the loo, so his mates leave the compartment so he can do his business in a bottle.

Three soldiers with impressive kepis come into our compartment in turns. One collects our passports, another one our customs declaration and a third one our exit cards. All electronic devices, books, magazines and phones must be declared. Currency too – but that is not checked.

Then a fourth one throws a cursory glance at our luggage and goes through our cameras. We all try to look cooperative; and quickly comply with whatever request they come up with. One soldier looks with great suspicion at Hong Kong Edward's little white camera recorder, but he has no idea how to handle it and so he relies on Edward's fabricated explanation. Fact is that the border guards cannot keep up with technology.

The other Hong Kong-er in our compartment makes the mistake of returning a phone call from his mobile during the border control inspection. As we are near the Chinese border we can use the Chinese network. One soldier sees him, and angrily asks him what he is doing. He snatches the phone from the Hong Kong-er's hand and goes through his messages and emails. You can hear a pin drop.

One person on the train is asked to delete a few photos. He does it, right in front of the soldier. What the soldier doesn't know is that there is a backup memory card in his shoe.

All of this takes the best part of four hours. All in all, the checking of our luggage and phones was more perfunctory than real. The repeated threats and warnings were far more successful in preserving the North Korean State, because it scared us into self-censorship.

The last soldier leaving our train manages a wry laconic smile.

The train starts moving.

We see a playground with dilapidated rides.

Three children look up at our dirty windows.

They don't smile.

The train moves over the bridge, towards the light.

We uncork the bottles.

We are free.

ANNEXE

Principles for Unitary Ideology of 1974, subsequently amended, which cemented the deification of the Great Leader.

1. Everyone must whole-heartedly struggle to remake the entire society into Kim Il-sung/Kim Jong-il-ism.

2. Everyone must highly revere Great Comrade Kim Il-sung and Comrade Kim Jong-il as Eternal Leader of the Workers' Party of Korea and people, and as the Sun of Juche.

3. Everyone must safeguard to death and accept as absolute the authority of Great Comrade Kim Il-sung and Comrade Kim Jong-il, as well as the Party's authority.

4. Everyone must absolutely arm the revolutionary ideology of Great Comrade Kim Il-sung and Comrade Kim Jong-il, as well as the Party's lines and policies which apply that ideology.

5. Everyone must absolutely observe the principles unconditionally in pursuing the teachings of Great Comrade Kim Il-sung and Comrade Kim Jong-il as well as the Party's lines and policies.

6.   Everyone must strengthen in every possible way the Party's ideological unity and revolutionary cohesion around the Leader.

7.   Everyone must learn after Great Comrade Kim Il-sung and Comrade Kim Jong-il and maintain refined mental and moral postures and revolutionary working methods, as well as people's working styles.

8.   Everyone must cherish the political life handed down by the Party and the Great Leader, and must repay the Party's trust and considerations with enhanced political self-respect and productive output.

9.   Everyone must build strong organisational rules so that the entire Party, the nation, and the military could move uniformly as one under the unitary leadership of the Party.

10.   To the end, everyone must succeed and complete the great task of Juche revolution and the great task of Military-first revolution that Great Comrade Kim Il-sung launched and Comrade Kim Jong-il implemented.

'A lie told often enough becomes the truth'

VLADIMIR LENIN

ACKNOWLEDGEMENTS

With special thanks (in no particular order) to: Alexandra Meaden, Matt Care, Joseph Meaden, Alex Hough, Lydia Ellis, Isaak Duffy, Robert Tollemache, Edward Chin, Nick Bustin, Michael Manning Clark, Lucinda Anstruther and Lester Waters. I hope I haven't forgotten anyone! They, my friends, read draft chapters, commented and made suggestions for improvements. Without honest feedback, no book is possible.

A warm thank you to the team at Biteback Publishing: Olivia Beattie, who accepted my book proposal; Alison MacDonald, who spent many days painstakingly brushing up my creaky English; Isabelle Ralphs, who dealt with the press; and Sam Jones, who very successfully marketed my book.

And above all, in North Korea: L., L. and K. who dared to talk to me, even when they were scared. You may never read this, but I will not forget you.

BIBLIOGRAPHY

Branigan, Tania, 'North Korea's Fashion Police', *The Guardian*, 24 April 2014.

Demick, Barbara, *Nothing to Envy*, Granta Books, 2010.

Evans, Stephen, 'Kidnapped by North Korea – and forced to make films', BBC Magazine, 27 February 2015.

Furnlanis, Ermanno, 'I made pizza for Kim Jong-il', *Asia Times*, 4 August 2001.

Gluckman, Ron, '90,000 ways to love a "great" leader', www.gluckman.com.

Harden, Blaine, *Escape from Camp 14*, Viking Books, March 2012.

Harrold, Michael, *Behind the Closed Doors of North Korea*, John Wiley & Sons, 2004.

Harrold, Michael, *Comrades and Strangers*, John Wiley & Sons, 2004.

Hassig, Ralph, and Oh, Kongdan, *The Hidden People of North Korea: Everyday Life in the Hermit Kingdom*, Rowman & Littlefield, 16 April 2015.

Hauter, Francois, 'Les captives étrangères de la Corée du Nord', *Le Figaro*, 21 April 2008.

Henry Jackson Society, 'The World's Most Closed Nation: Exposing Crimes against Humanity in North Korea', 25 April 2012.

Hitchens, Christopher, 'Visit to a small planet', *Vanity Fair*, 14 August 2008.

Jang, Jin-sung, *Dear Leader*, Ebury Publishing, 2014.

Johnson, Adam, 'Dear Leader dreams of sushi', *GQ*, 3 June 2013.

Kim, Chae Hwan, 'Residents ordered to gather and follow Party Congress on TV', *Daily NK*, 6 May 2016.

Kim, Hyun Hee, *The Tears of my Soul*, William Morrow & Co., October 1993.

Kim, Narae, 'North Korea says apartment building collapses', Reuters, 18 May 2014.

Kim, Ok Sun, *Kim Jong Suk, The Anti-Japanese Heroine*, Foreign Languages Publishing House, 1997.

Kim, Soo, 'Inside the luxury world of Kim Jong-un', *Daily Telegraph*, 27 August 2015.

Koonse, Emma, 'North Korean defector who spent 28 years in prison camp details hunger, torture, and aannibalism in the DPRK', *Christian Post*, 6 May 2015.

Korea Institute for National Unification, White Paper on Human Rights in North Korea 2014.

Lankov, Andrei, 'Bomb in Ryongchon?', *Korea Times*, 1 June 2014.

Lankov, Andrei, *The Real North Korea*, Oxford University Press, 2014.

Law, Diane, *The Secret History of the Great Dictators*, Constable & Robinson Ltd, 2009.

Lee, Ye Son, 'Ask a North Korean: Do you drink alcohol?', *The Guardian*, 14 December 2015.

Martin, Bradley K., *Under the Loving Care of the Fatherly Leader*, Thomas Dunne Books, 2004.

Meuser, Philipp, *Architectural and Cultural Guide: Pyongyang*, Dom Publishers, 15 March 2012.

Miyoshi Jager, *Sheila, Brothers at War*, Profile Books, 2013.

Park, Ju-he, 'Williams Joyce, Private ownership of land now legal in North Korea', *New Focus*, 28 June 2016.

Park, Ju-Min, 'Asia's hottest property market is also its most unlikely: North Korea', Reuters, 25 March 2014.

Pattison, Pete, 'North Koreans working as "state-sponsored slaves" in Qatar', *The Guardian*, 7 November 2014.

Quackenbush, Casey, 'Architect of gleaming new North Korea airport missing after leader notes "defects"', *The Observer*, 17 September 2015.

Shim, Elizabeth, 'North Korea scientists live in lavish apartments for free, Pyongyang says', *United Press International*, 17 November 2015.

Soukhorukov, Sergey, 'Train blast "was a plot to kill North Korea's leader"', *Daily Telegraph*, 13 June 2004.

Tertitskiy, Fyodor, 'The day Kim Il-sung died his first death', *Asia Times*, 25 September 2013.

Truong, Alice, 'A gap year like no other', Quartz, 1 August 2015.

Wainwright, Oliver, 'The Pyonghattan project: how North Korea's capital is transforming into a "socialist fairyland"', *The Guardian*, 11 September 2015.

Weissman, Jordan, 'How Kim Jong-il starved North Korea', *Atlantic Monthly*, 20 December 2011.

Williams, Rob, 'North Korean cannibalism fears amid claims starving people forced to desperate measures', *The Independent*, 28 January 2013.

Yong, Lee Sang, 'Apartments on Mirae Scientists' Street "frozen solid"', *Daily NK*, 29 January 2016.

INDEX